CHRISTOPHER CORNTHWAITE

Doctoring

Building a Life With a PhD

First edition

This book was professionally typeset on Reedsy.
Find out more at reedsy.com

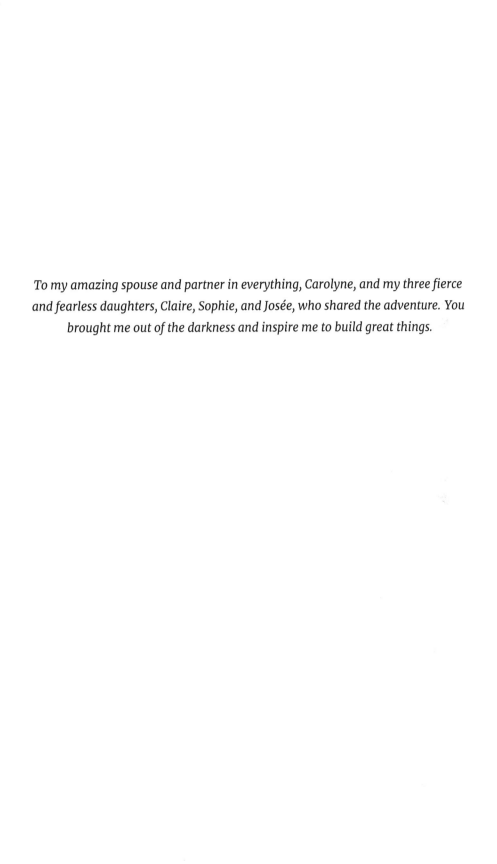

To my amazing spouse and partner in everything, Carolyne, and my three fierce and fearless daughters, Claire, Sophie, and Josée, who shared the adventure. You brought me out of the darkness and inspire me to build great things.

Contents

Preface

This is a book for PhDs. To many who have not spent time in the academy, the fact that there needs to be a book talking about how to build a life with the highest degree you can get might be shocking. *Doesn't a better degree mean a better job?* they might ask. *Why would you do a six-year degree and have no job at the other end?*

If you're doing, have done, or are thinking of doing a PhD, you know that the answer is more complicated. PhDs are facing record high un- and underemployment within the academy. Most PhDs still expect to be professors, yet there are virtually a handful of jobs each year for thousands of new graduates. Many of us are struggling to hold on to precarious adjunct contracts. We are watching the university eliminate the very positions we are spending five to ten years training for as we are training.

I began to write this book in January of 2020. In March of 2020, we were hit with the biggest pandemic in at least a century, and it shows no signs of stopping yet. As I write this, countries around the world are still struggling to contain it. "Social distancing," a term I had never heard before, is now on everyone's lips.

The situation in the academy before the pandemic was already bad. By the time this is over, it may perhaps be far worse. Someone may say the virus killed academia. The reality for those of us who finished our degrees before the virus is that this pandemic was just the latest event in a long string of collapses within the academy that have been happening for decades.

I don't know what the future will hold for the academy. I hear a lot of doom and gloom, but it is entirely possible things may get better. Whether they get better or worse, this book is not primarily about the university system. You and I are limited in our ability to change the academic situation. But we are endlessly powerful to change our own situations. That's what I want to talk to you about, and I hope hearing my story may help you on your own journey.

At the end of the day, I don't want to be hamstrung by the potential ups and downs of academia, or a non-academic job for that matter. I want to create a life and career that has tremendous value in any market. I want a career that thrives regardless of the good fortunes of a higher-ed budget decision or hiring committee. I hope you'll dream this dream with me, and step boldly into your own future. You have a gift to offer the world, something great to do. I don't know what it is, but I know that we need your voice and your talents. So, whether you've forgotten who you are, or you just need to know where to go next, this book will challenge your thinking.

It can seem hard to generalize about PhDs. From different countries, disciplines, programs, and backgrounds, everyone has vastly unique experiences of studying. My experience as a humanities student is not the same as someone in STEM. Yet, as I've learned from blogging about this, there are also similarities winding through all of our stories. There are similar frustrations that many of us face, regardless of our background.

No matter where you're from or which degree you've done, you can build a great life and career from it. But it's not an easy road. These are lessons I've learned on mine.

I

Rescuing Yourself

1

LOST AND FOUND

The Greek island of Syros is a tiny dot in the Mediterranean, close to the more-popular holiday island of Mykonos. Its rolling brown hills and white houses rise out of the sparkling blue water like a whale's back, and the only disruption to the sleepy island life is when the enormous ferry pulls into the port three times a day, blasting its horn and creating a traffic jam for miles around.

My family and I were on Syros for a vacation. Our white villa with the quintessential blue shutters sat on the top of a hill looking out over the rolling water, and I could see the island of Rhenia in the distance, where archaeologists found some of the ancient, Greek inscriptions that made it into my PhD thesis. I studied "religions of Mediterranean antiquity," which is a fancy way of saying Greek and Roman religion. This included Christianity. I tried to track how different religions spread through diaspora communities, looking for comparisons to the spread of Christianity so I could understand if and how Jewish communities hosted the new religion.

I was vaguely aware that I should probably be over there peering through the ruins and trying to contribute something to both human knowledge and my dissertation, but this was vacation. My thesis was half done, and I was tired of academia.

I initially came to Greece with high hopes of getting in on archaeological digs and exploring the ancient sites for Greek inscriptions that told the story of these ancient immigrants. But I was realizing that all of the extra archaeological work wouldn't make a difference to my ability to find an academic job, so I decided to focus on enjoying Greece instead. I was exhausted by the academic fight, and my soul had lost the spark that drew me to study in the first place.

It was late September and the island was quiet, the tourists were disappearing. We wandered down to the beach below the villa and the kids made sandcastles and splashed in the salty water, still warm by Canadian standards. We hiked the rocky trails on the capes around our villa, picking up interesting rocks and shells and bringing them home. The girls stumbled into a flock of goats and they clamored around us hoping for food as my daughters squealed with delight.

We walked the quiet roads through the deserted countryside into the nearest town for food and groceries. This town had its own deserted beach with a couple of white hotels sitting on it. They were preparing to close for the winter, but still served us and the few other stragglers who hadn't taken the hint that this was no longer Greek summer. We sat on beach chairs and drank Freddo Cappuccino, then wandered up for dinner to eat mouth-watering gyros and souvlaki slathered in tzatziki.

One evening, we sat in the now-deserted restaurant near a retired American couple, who overheard us speaking English and stopped to chat. We exchanged pleasantries and they told us they were from San Francisco. We chatted for a few minutes. I explained that I was a researcher; my work was on a nearby island, but we were vacationing right now.

Then, the lady said something that's always stuck with me: "It sounds like you live a charmed life."

Charmed life.

That was an interesting way to say it. It wasn't wrong. I could feel the truth in it — to an outside observer, we were in paradise. And we were.

But I was in internal turmoil. I had just finished some job applications for another academic job-rejection season, and I was feeling down on myself. Even in this beautiful place, I felt empty. My sense of direction was imploding quickly, and I was facing the fact that I was probably not going to be a professor.

Back in our little villa, I connected to Wi-Fi and pored over the academic job postings, waiting for one that fit. Carolyne, my spouse, sat reading on the couch. The kids were in bed.

One by one, I read the postings to her from my laptop: "What do you think about a postdoc in Durham? We could make that work, right? It pays £15,000, but isn't UK money twice what ours is?"

She smiled at me, knowing how hard this was. "Sure honey. We might be able to make that work."

I thought of how ludicrous it was that I was even *thinking* of applying to drag my family to a new country for one year to make $30,000 Canadian — about the same as I'd made working part-time for a non-profit years before.

I looked up cost-of-living on Numbeo. "Oh, that wouldn't even cover our rent. Never mind."

I went back to scanning. "How about a visiting professor gig in California? California could be fun!"

She smiled again, and I thought of moving our kids — then three, five, and six — to a new place again for one year, to make no money, only to have to start over again a year later. Sure, we were nomads living in Greece. But that felt different. It was part of my research and it was easy to understand that it was for a time. We were ready to start real life, and we wanted to be settled.

I was slowly realizing that Greece was one last fun adventure for my PhD, but that it would be the end of my road. And it was a hell of a way to go out, really.

* * *

Approximately fifty-five thousand PhDs will graduate in America this year, and about six thousand in Canada.[1] According to Statista's figures on PhDs graduating worldwide from 2014, the UK, Germany, and India each graduate about twenty-five thousand a year, while Australia produces about eight thousand.[2] Each of them are going through a similar thought process to the one I went through (*some* in India seem to do a little better, anecdotally). Most came into academia with the hopes of getting the golden goose: a tenure track job. Most — perhaps as many as 90 percent — will never see a tenure-track job, and this number seems to be dropping every year.[3]

These PhDs will all go through the same dance that I went through. Each person has their own characteristics and non-negotiables to consider. Few will love the options they get. Most will try to figure out if they can make it work. If they can survive on the money. If they can afford rent. If their level of physical ability will be accommodated. If they'll be belittled and talked down to by senior profs.

It's a balancing act nobody should have to do at the end of an advanced degree. Students rarely have jobs they're excited about to choose from (although there are usually some to apply to). More frequently, they must consider what they're willing to sacrifice. They must gauge how much longer they're willing to play the game, and whether it's worth the gamble.

Many of us who have spent enough time in the education system know how bad things are. Master's graduates who got out and resisted pressure to do a PhD — many of whom are now employed in really cool jobs — often see the PhD as something they escaped. Some master's graduates resent PhDs.

When I meet a PhD who's killing it in the real world, we usually share a few moments at the beginning of the conversation to shake our heads about the current state of education. When I tell my story, starting with, "I applied for tenure-track jobs, but didn't get one," they smile knowingly, as if to say, *Yes, we are in agreement. The university is a shit show, and we're glad we're not there anymore.*

The bigger question may be why nobody is *doing* anything about it. Why do universities keep accepting students to degrees that are essentially vocational training for the professoriate, why do governments keep funding the degrees, and why would anyone want to do one? This is a more complicated question that I've only begun to understand.

In 2018, I was running policy projects for a Canadian think tank. I sat at a roundtable of Canada's who's who. Some elegant sandwiches sat off to the side, and the twenty people around the table included former cabinet ministers, CEOs, leaders in Crown corporations and government, and somebody high up in university leadership in Canada. I won't divulge the latter's identity — I'll just call him Mr. University.

The topic of the roundtable was how to make Canada's economy competitive.

My ears perked up when I heard the issue of education and skills-training come up, one close to my own heart because of my arduous journey out of the PhD. Even now, although I was making $70,000 — significantly better than most postdocs I could have been doing — I was sitting at the table as a project organizer and not a subject-matter expert. I was aware of the irony that I was one of the most-educated people at the table and, although I was welcome to give input, I didn't feel qualified to. These were leaders in their industries who had spent years learning by doing. I had an esoteric degree and had studied weird stuff that was useless at that table.

Plus, I didn't trust my own voice. It took a lot of humility to go and take a job organizing events for these important people. I had to swallow my pride, a lot. Coming out of academia hurt my confidence, and I didn't believe that what I had to say was credible. It would take time to repair that confidence.

But then, sitting next to me, Mr. University leaned back in his chair with a smug smile on his face and said, "Well, we've got no problems with training. Our universities are doing a fantastic job of training young people for the workforce. We're advanced and competitive..."

I wanted to scream. When was the last time he'd spoken to an actual graduate student about what things were really like? I imagined jumping on the table and delivering a powerful monologue to the assembled there about what a disaster higher ed as I knew it was.

Are you kidding!? I would say. I've spent seventeen years in higher ed, and I'm starting all over again from the beginning of my career, no further ahead than I was a decade ago. I'm here organizing your roundtables and arranging your sandwiches. And at least I have a paycheck. There are thousands of students who don't, or who are working at Starbucks, 'because it has benefits.' YOU ARE FAILING! You are failing the students you claim to represent, and the brightest minds of our time are languishing in underemployment.

And you want to talk about economic growth? The Canadian government spent

HUNDREDS *of thousands of dollars to educate me in a field that doesn't exist* *anymore. They poured MILLIONS into the work of my profs, to train students* *for academic jobs that don't exist anymore.* DO YOU THINK THIS IS A GOOD *INVESTMENT IN OUR FUTURE?!* DO YOU THINK THIS IS WHAT MAKES AN *ECONOMY COMPETITIVE?!*

I imagined everyone cheering, and the assembled powerful people rushing back to their offices to make appropriate changes to the education system and fix the status quo.

But I didn't say anything. I bit my tongue and sat nodding and typing into my computer.

The good, obedient PhD.

* * *

Meanwhile, as optimistic as Mr. University was about the effectiveness of our graduate programs, one finds a very different outlook on university campuses. There's a sense of doom settling over many university departments. Students who were wined and dined on PhD departmental tours and campus visits end up plunging into a communal malaise as they enter programs only to be profoundly disappointed.

The hushed whispers can begin as early as the first year. The people who recruited you have gone quiet about the department and the great options. The professors who talked a good game about how well their students are doing outside of academia now won't have that conversation anymore.

Everyone's afraid. And sad. Collectively depressed.

In the fourth year of my PhD, as I was beginning to write up my research and think about applying for academic jobs, I saw a colleague at a conference who I'd sort of known from years earlier. He was walking by — rushed — and I called to him. I reminded him who I was.

He looked like he'd been running from someone, and with a desperate look on his face said, "Do you know of any jobs?"

I was taken aback, not quite sure of how to answer. This was a scholar who I respected a lot. He was further in his journey than me; I knew him while he was doing a prestigious postdoc. I'd cited his monograph frequently in my dissertation. And he was scared. He was desperate enough to ask a PhD student he barely knew if I knew of jobs he could apply for.

* * *

These two montages tell two different stories. Senior decision-makers most often hear from senior administrative people in universities and their lobbying groups. As such, they don't hear about the carnage that is happening in graduate programs. The university does powerful government relations to keep the system *status quo* and to keep things moving as they are. Why wouldn't they?

The administrative system (at least up until the pandemic) has been benefiting from the current system. The explosion of support and managerial staff at universities, in some cases far outpacing the growth of faculty hires, means that there is more administration at universities than full-time professors.[4] It's their story of the university that government hears, and it is not in their interests to tell a negative one. They have more job security than the thousands of adjunct professors who deliver the core education of the university.

On the other hand, PhD students are lost and desperate, convinced that they have no future (an assumption that is confirmed every way they look). They are depressed and struggling with serious mental-health challenges — as *Nature* recently uncovered.[5] And the government that funds the universities often does not hear these stories.

So, what is the PhD problem?

Ironically, to most outsiders there isn't a problem. PhDs in Canada and the United States do fine in the non-academic labor market, usually out-earning their peers with master's degrees after a few years.[6] To an untrained observer, this is hardly a cause for concern. A PhD still seems to have real labor-market value, and for this reason it's difficult to get policymakers to take PhDs seriously as a lost cause. In fact, I agree. PhDs do well in the "real world;" they earn a lot and do neat jobs.

So, the better question might be: Is there a PhD problem?

While there are many that I'll talk about in the book, perhaps the greatest problem is a gap between expectations and reality, which is rooted in university culture. While it's always changing as universities grapple with the realities of the academic job market, many departments and professors still associate a negative stigma with any type of non-academic work. This can be either a spoken or unspoken belief that academic jobs are superior, that often filters students' sense of where their careers should go.

However, the stigma does not only come from the professorial rank. One of the beliefs that consistently shows up is that students expect to be tenure-track professors. A Canadian study found that over 60 percent of PhD students entering their studies expected to become tenured university professor (with some variation for field). Less than 20 percent actually will.[7]

But despite these dismal chances, students keep enrolling in graduate degrees, and many keep ignoring non-academic career options until, frankly, they're desperate.

There are different factors that push students into graduate school while simultaneously discouraging a student from thinking about building a non-academic career with a graduate degree.

Systemic Factors

- Undergraduate and graduate mentors tell students they should go to grad school because of their talent.
- Many programs naturally privilege and idealize graduate studies as a logical next step for talented undergrads.
- Universities actively recruit for graduate programs, even knowing that there are no career options.
- Our society socializes students to equate education and degrees with career success.
- Social discourse around education considers university the superior educational option to other pathways, like vocational training.

Familial/Cultural Factors

- Parents teach children that a degree equals a good job — especially blue-collar parents who understand post-secondary as a means to escape their own lot in life.
- Some students are the first in their family to attend higher ed, or even among the first in their programs from under-represented groups. They consider themselves trailblazers in spaces that have not typically welcomed them, and their academic success is therefore symbolic of progress within a hostile system.

Personal factors

- The student doesn't know what else to do and has no career direction.
- The student is used to achieving at a high level and believes that they will beat the odds to land the tenure-track professor job.
- The student holds the misconception that they need a more advanced degree to build a career.
- The student does not have adequate career-building support after their first degrees, or does not access what's there (university career centers, etc.)
- The student believes that graduate studies are uniquely meaningful and will help them achieve some sort of idealistic higher calling in life.

When one combines the self-delusion of graduate departments with general ignorance among PhDs about the probabilities and possibilities of actually working as a tenure-track professor, we begin to see why so many will face a considerable let down during and after their doctorates.

Now universities are scrambling to talk about what a great job their graduates are doing finding work outside of academia. They're talking about transferable skills and hosting seminars on how to get non-academic jobs. They have realized that they need to offer these resources to keep students coming in the door.

But you know what? The majority of PhD students don't come to study for non-academic jobs. If you said to a potential PhD recruit, "You WILL NOT get an academic job, but come do your PhD as a training for a non-academic job you could get with your bachelor's degree," more potential students would run the other way. And rightly so.

The tenure-track dream, even in the current state of academia, is still the carrot on a stick that many departments use to get students to enroll. They'll talk about non-academic work as "plan B," even though most current or recent graduates will have to go this way. But students have big dreams, dreams that serve universities well and keep pumping out research. So, they keep doing what they've always done. If you're a PhD, this is done at the expense of your financial well-being, your career, and your sanity.

* * *

This will not be a book about how bad academia is. I'm guessing if you're reading this you probably know how bad it is and are more interested in how you can make a career out of your degree. Perhaps you are still in academia and hoping to rescue a life from your PhD. Perhaps you've already left and are struggling.

That's where I was. I realized that everyone's scared — and it can feel like nobody's listening. There's a lot about the system that's fucked up. Yup. I'll just say that. But getting mad at how fucked it is isn't going to help you much. At the end of the day, you're an individual. Nobody's going to fight for your future like you can. Maybe it's time to stop waiting for the system to change and save you and start rescuing yourself. You need to do what's right for your health. You might need an income soon, and maybe you have dependents to support. Maybe you just want to gain back your self-esteem.

For all of us there comes a time when we have to end something that we hoped would be great. There comes a time to burn it down and walk away. No, I don't mean burn down the university — even if it's tempting some days. I'm talking about burning down the dream.

It's hard to let go of that tenure-track dream.

You have one, don't you? My tenure-track dream Chris worked at Oxford or Cambridge. For a Canadian kid who grew up steeped in English culture, these schools appealed to me more than the Ivies. Tenure-track Chris sits around in old coffee shops and goes to a thousand-year-old pub with colleagues for fish and chips. Tenure-track Chris teaches engaged students in an old, stone classroom, and then swings by the Bodleian library to look at ancient manuscripts. Tenure-track Chris keeps a sailboat harbored in the Mediterranean, Crete probably, and he uses it to trace the paths of the ancient sailors that he writes about.

Tenure-track you may look different from tenure-track me, but I'm guessing that they exist. They are the figment of your tenure-track dream that you've been chasing for a long time. You've sunk a lot of time and hope into tenure-track you. I get it.

And I'm not going to tell you when it's time to burn it down and walk away. That would be presumptuous of me. How would I know what's right for you? It was hard enough to figure out when it was time for me to stick a ceremonial sword through tenure-track Chris.

But somewhere in the endless cycle of rejected job applications, meeting great senior people who couldn't get hired, and thinking through moving my family to rural Texas for eight months, I woke up. I realized that my tenure-track self was actually getting me hurt. It was making me consider some very bad decisions in hopes that I might inch a bit closer to that tenure-track dream.

Finally, there came a day when I faced the truth:

I'm not going to get a good academic job.

And my internal voice screamed back:

Hold on one more year, you never know!

The market will pick up!

The postdoc is a stepping-stone to where you want to be.

There was the cruel truth of the academic job cycle — that I *might* have gotten a job. But is that worth years of my life? Is that slim possibility worth ruining my financial future and dragging my family through hell? Is it worth feeling worthless all the time?

For me, it was not.

I miss tenure-track Chris, and I occasionally wish I could reanimate him. But like Frankenstein's monster, he wouldn't be what he seems in my imagination. I didn't leave because I didn't like academia. I left because I had no future there. Tenure-track Chris could never exist in academia as it stands.

You might look back once you're gone, too. We all do now and then, don't we? We're so scared of regret and stepping off the path we're on.

But what if I told you you're going to spend the next ten years as an adjunct or visiting prof, you'll keep being impoverished, and wind up even more lost and desperate than you are now? Would that be worth holding on to?

In the end, I didn't make the decision to leave based on what might happen. I saw the PhD grads who were years ahead of me, and I knew that what *might* happen wasn't going to happen. Or at least, there wasn't enough chance of it happening for me to keep holding on. In fact, there was not one tenure-track job in my field in Canada the year I left.

I made the right decision. The figments that make up my tenure-track self can be taken apart and brought to life in other ways. I could still live around the world, teach people, and even flit around Greece or sail the Mediterranean. I just had to find different ways to make that dream a reality.

So, where are you? If you know it's time, maybe you need to burn it down and walk away. Stick the sword through your tenure-track self or bash them over the head with a ceremonial mace. Or—if you don't want to be that dramatic—just put them in the cupboard for a little bit and try some things. You might be surprised by what you find. It's possible to change your path and thrive.

The chapters that follow are not about giving you a list of non-academic jobs you can get. Part one is devoted to repairing the damage that academia has done to your sense of self worth and recapturing the dream again. It reflects on feeling lost and directionless after leaving academia and offers a roadmap to rediscovering yourself and your vision.

Part two is devoted to life and career lessons that I've learned, including building leadership skills, a network, and a personal brand, while learning to think about what it takes to build the career you want.

Throughout the book, I'll share stories of reinvention, both my own and others', and I hope you'll be both challenged and inspired by the possibilities for your degree. This book is not about how bad academia is. It's about how great reinvention can be and how to do it.

2

WHAT CAN YOU DO WITH A PHD?

The question of what you can do with a PhD is one that dogs a lot of people who are pursuing them. The best departments are filled with professors who mean well, but may not have any idea of what you can actually do with a PhD outside of academia. The worst ones have cultures of shame around PhDs in non-academic work. They may gaslight PhDs who are worried about their future, making them think that they need to commit more or stop considering life outside of academia. Because of this, many PhDs don't realize that they will likely be working outside of academia. If they do, they have no idea where to start.

The good news is that, as academia closes for PhDs, the non-academic world is opening. More of us are entering the non-academic workplace, both by choice and by necessity. For those PhDs who are willing to be open-minded, to learn on their feet, to take roles that help them build, and to try their best to understand the world, anything is possible.

I once posted an inspirational saying on Twitter that suggested anything is possible for people with advanced degrees. Someone sarcastically responded that they want to be President of the United States. This seemed like a joke to that person, but I don't know why it should be. Senator Elizabeth Warren — an academic — ran for the nomination in the Democratic primary. It should be clear that it is POSSIBLE for academics to run for office. And the possibilities don't stop there. Former Secretary of State Condoleezza Rice has a PhD in military history and policy. Actress Mayim Bialik has a PhD in neuroscience from UCLA. TV host Rachel Maddow has a PhD in politics from Oxford.

Because PhDs are often socialized to view non-academic work as a failure, we sometimes lack the vision to see how incredible life with a PhD outside of academia can be. We dream so small, thinking that by leaving academia we must shrink our dreams and settle. The irony is that, for many PhDs I know working outside, academia would be too small to hold them. They would feel constrained by it. And with time, I've come to believe the same thing about myself. A tenure-track position is not a big enough container for my dreams.

I won't ever give a list of things you can do with a PhD. You can do anything that doesn't require a professional designation or a skill set you can't learn.

I certainly never saw any of the roles I've had on a "jobs" list for religious studies PhDs. Yet as I jumped into new roles, I discovered new possibilities for my career. Each time I was hired, I became a student of those workplaces. During my first month of non-academic work at the think tank, I had to sit in front of $100,000 budgets and figure out how to assign all the parts of the whole. I worked with clients on great ideas. I learned how the government worked.

But the most important lesson I learned was that I saw how ideas become money — a vital thing for former academics to understand. It seemed to happen out of thin air. The president of the think tank I worked for would go out for lunch with someone and come back with $50,000 for a new research project. Coming from a world of people who had great ideas living mostly in poverty, this was a vital process to understand.

My personal network exploded too, and I saw just how important networking was. This is why I'm such a proponent of networking for career building. Every coffee I'd have with someone could have thousands of dollars riding on it. From associations to government to unions to corporate Canada, everyone was looking to spend money on great research projects. Everyone wanted to fund things. Nobody wanted to be left out of a great idea. If the latest research project on education and skills or immigration went forward, organizations would be terrified that their names would be left off the lists. They desperately wanted to be a part of it.

Ideas became money. Relationships became power and access. And I became mentally stronger, certain of the tremendous opportunities that existed. I grew confident, even arrogant at the possibilities sometimes.

I began to realize that, with some time and foresight, I could not only get employed, but I could actually use my social power and my voice to shape my country into something that I wanted it to be. I had the ability to look at enormous social problems and join in the fight to fix them. Everywhere I looked, I met PhDs doing just this, shaping our country with their skills and knowledge, and it became my vision too.

Most PhDs I talk to think that things are happening TO them, and at first this can be true. But over time, with enough drive and creativity, you can see things happening FOR you as well. This, my friend, is the sweet spot in life: when you can look at the world and create there what you think should exist. Maybe you own a company or maybe you work for one, but when you operate in a field knowing what it needs and how to make it happen, you can speak into the void and watch things come to life.

Incidentally, this is the same thing that professors do. They look at the research environment and create projects out of thin air, applying to funding bodies to make the projects happen. The best professors don't just make their salary; they create tremendous wealth and value for their universities, bringing in thousands and millions of dollars in external funding.

This is the real power of the PhD. Once you learn how the non-academic world works — and there is a learning curve — you can apply your intelligence, your project management skills, and your leadership capabilities to almost any social problem. Combined with a world-creating spirit, you can produce anything you want. Because the PhD is a ticket to create, even outside of academia. People who work in a knowledge economy fully expect to see PhDs leading things, running projects, creating companies, filing patents, or joining startups. More and more, PhDs are entering the workplace as visionary leaders, smart and confident and ready to take on the world. Having those letters after your name might do little for you by themselves. But having the letters after your name when you're a world creator, even outside of the academy, just maximizes your ability to create. People take you seriously.

So, let me save you the trouble of Googling, "what can you do with a PhD?" The answer is, WHATEVER THE FUCK YOU WANT. The better question to ask yourself is, "What do I want to do? What world do I want to create?"

* * *

I know that you may be reading this as someone who has applied for — what seems like — a million jobs and had a million rejections. You are broken and tired — tired of being told that you're overqualified and tired of begging for table scraps of jobs that you can't even get.

I need you to look deep inside yourself and find a spark of greatness that is about to be extinguished. Somewhere in your destroyed soul there used to live a little spark of hopefulness, even excitement about the future. Somewhere in there, there's a first-year PhD student who thought that this PhD path was the most exciting thing to ever happen to them. Somehow, what seemed like a world of possibilities disappeared along with the dream of tenure-track you, and you would be willing to settle for a decent position at Starbucks to make rent.

Look inside and find that little flame that used to be there. Find the nugget of a dream that once lived in your soul. And start to fan it again. Don't worry about building a resume yet. Don't apply for jobs. Just focus on finding that little part of you that once believed that the world was your oyster and start to nourish it again. That's what needs to come first. You need to begin to believe that to have the ability to do great things and revive your ability to dream.

Then, recognize that you are a world creator. And ask yourself what kind of world you want to create. Maybe you want to create a world with no poverty. Maybe, as I watched one PhD decide recently, you want to create a world where children are safe from exploitation. Maybe, like another PhD I know, you want to bring science to underprivileged kids.

When I began to fan this flame again in my heart, I eventually realized what I wanted to use my world-creating power for. I wanted to strive to create better outcomes for students. This meant PhD students, of course, where a lot of my efforts are still focused. But it also meant students with other degrees that felt useless. In fact, most of my siblings had done various arts and humanities degrees in their undergrad and were underemployed.

Instead of sitting around waiting for policymakers to change things, what if the students had information about how to create great careers? Most of the work I've read suggests that agency is one of the most powerful factors in determining student outcomes.[8] So what if we empowered students to take control of their own lives and careers? What if we taught them how to navigate through the graduate education system, and especially out of it? If we had a world where students were empowered to do this, we could diminish the crisis in higher education.

The answer that stuck in my head, as I immersed myself in non-academic work, was simply that people needed stories. Students needed to be empowered to dig themselves out of the various messes they were in; exploitative relationships, crappy adjunct positions, mountains of debt, or whatever challenge they were facing. Because nobody else was going to do it for them.

Since starting Roostervane, I've heard stories from people all over the world, many of whom are being horribly mistreated by academia. I've heard of supervisors stealing research, students being physically, sexually, emotionally, and otherwise assaulted and abused by colleagues or mentors. I've heard about funding being indiscriminately cut off, students being kicked out of programs without cause, students following their professors across the country or the world in desperate bids to keep their funding and finish their degrees (that would otherwise be lost).

There are so many terrible stories. Each seems more horrific than the last, but at the same time, we become numb to them after a while. The horrendous nature of academia becomes like a sad running joke for people that go through it. Everyone knows that academia eats its young, but nobody's fixing it. And I wondered if I could be a part of the solution. This was what I wanted to use my world-creating power for.

What will you do with yours?

* * *

The irony landed on me after I left academia. PhDs who stepped outside were doing very well. When I was still in, the desperation and fear weighed heavy. Once I started working outside and realizing how much I could do with those three letters after my name, I wondered why more people didn't leave.

When I was a kid, I loved the book *The Last Battle* by C.S. Lewis. In one scene in the book, people are being thrown into a stable as an offering for the god Tash. To everyone's surprise, after fighting to avoid being thrown into the dark stable, there is another world inside—another reality. The battle is taking place at night, but as they step into the stable, the protagonists see the green grass and the bright sky; they are in the middle of a meadow.

But there was also a group of dwarves who were thrown into the stable, who didn't believe that this other reality was possible. In their minds, they were still in the dark stable. So, they sat huddled in what they thought was the darkness, when they were actually in a wide-open field. They refused to be fooled, and to avoid believing that a better world was possible and present, they stayed trapped in the prison of their mind.

Sometimes, I think some of those still in academia are like the dwarves sitting in the middle of that field. All around are possibilities to be happy — a big, beautiful world that needs their talent and energy — but they sit in a tiny circle refusing to believe that anything else is possible. They won't look up and see the sun or the sky.

I'm not trying to blame students. It's not our fault we were socialized to think about academia the way that we have been. But, at the same time, we don't need to sit in darkness either. Stories of those who have successfully left academia and built great lives used to be rare. We can begin to tell these stories more and more, especially with easy access of social media.

Little by little, the light will begin to dawn. Although it's true that for many PhDs, being a professor is the only role that *requires* a PhD, there are an endless number of careers that you can get into. The job possibilities for PhDs become anything that requires problem solving, critical thinking, and leadership. Here are just a handful of PhDs who inspired me and showed what was possible.

Paul graduated with a PhD a decade ago, and in the last ten years has become a respected public opinion researcher. He built his own polling company from the ground up. When there's an election, it seems like I can't turn on the TV or radio without seeing him.

Kim is in leadership at one of Canada's top think tanks. She sits at the intersection of powerful politicians and government and leads projects that shape the future of my country. As I was finishing my own PhD and stalling with the defense, she would encourage me to finish and put it behind me. Jane has a PhD in medieval studies and runs a multimillion-dollar research portfolio in the think tank space.

James took his humanities PhD and launched into a career in the Canadian government. When I asked him what it was like to work in government, he told me, "The higher up you go, the smarter the people you get to hang around with. Government has a reputation for being 'dead wood', but the reality is that some of the sharpest minds in the country are here." Marie also works in the government. She's earlier in her career than James but is on her way to the top.

Jim is a PhD in anthropology who teaches part-time as an adjunct and leads user experience research for a big company. Pedro helps lead a biotech startup that just received a huge batch of funding. He's creating cancer-killing technology that will save lives. Asa works for a clean energy startup and her work fights climate change. Jenny runs a user experience program for Google. Phil works as a director of policy in the office of a cabinet minister.

Then there are the subject-matter expert PhDs that I've met. They work for everybody and nobody, cobbling together six-figure salaries from a mixture of positions that could be anything from consulting for government, holding fellowships at major think tanks, or offering their expertise to a government relations organization (AKA lobbying firm). Each of them is a one-person company, and the mere mention of their name in research circles is synonymous with expertise in their given area. When they release a report, people take it seriously.

Each of these people, and many more, have charted amazing life courses with their advanced degrees. And you can too. Here's what will happen if you leave. You will take yourself and your skills out into the beautiful world.

For a time, probably at least a few months and perhaps as long as a couple of years, you will struggle to find your way. It's an almost ubiquitous experience, especially for those of us who never thought we'd have to work outside of academia.

There will come a day when you will realize, just as I did, that the world is yours for the taking. That will mean different things depending on where you end up. In a big government city like Ottawa, it might mean networking your way through the halls of power to create the social change you want to see in the towns and cities (and especially universities) across Canada. You might do the same thing in Washington, London, Berlin, or Canberra. You might go to Silicon Valley, or an equivalent tech hub, and help build the future. You might work with the United Nations or a similar global organization and solve the grand challenges of our age. You may work in the ad industry in New York City, or perhaps the film industry in Hollywood. Or last, but certainly not least, you may decide to settle in a small town somewhere and fight for its well-being. You'll launch a business. You'll run for mayor.

You will watch the world unfold before you and you will see more options than you can imagine. And perhaps, if you're anything like most PhDs I know, there will come a day when you won't miss academia. Or, there may come a day when you decide to go and adjunct — not as a poor student with no options, but as a successful leader who wants to give back. Whatever path you take, you can do almost anything you choose with a PhD.

3

THE DARKNESS

In February of 2019, I was in a bad place. I spent most mornings sitting motionless in my chair, staring out the window wanting to cry. Believe it or not, I'd already worked a great job for the think tank. I'd met senators and cabinet ministers and CEOs and worked with an impressive network of Canadian leaders.

Then I struck out on my own to start a consulting career. In my big, wild dream, I envisioned starting a think tank. I'd worked in a think tank, and it was great. But I saw a lack of good research in the Canadian think tank space and a lot of rushed, half-assed projects. A dream began to form in my mind. What if we took all the underemployed PhDs and started training them to do public policy? What if we created a bridging program from academia to public policy that would train PhDs as policy leaders and, while we're at it, create a solid research-based policy shop with some of the brightest minds in Canada?

That was the dream. And I quit my think tank job with a vague plan and jumped out on my own. I started selling and putting a pitch sheet in front of people. It was a good idea — I still think it is. But my fear kicked in.

There's not much in this world that you can't conquer if you can conquer your own fear. I had a list of excuses I made that stopped me from going after my dream with everything I had:

I'm not good enough.

I don't have enough experience.

Who am I to be a CEO of something?

And the negative self-talk turned into another idea, a toxic ball of fear and anxiety that wrapped itself around my brain and wouldn't let me focus on anything else.

What if I'm not done with academia?

I didn't ever realize that I was operating under the fear of failure, but that's what it was. I told myself that I was being very rational, and that if I left academia behind, I couldn't come back. Was I sure this was a door I wanted to close?

My terrified mind screamed at me:

Maybe you're not done with academia! If you close this door, you can't go back through it. You actually LOVE doing research in ancient history; you only sort of like running policy projects.

I regressed. I had failed to get a tenure-track job, so I labelled myself a failure in other areas too. And without even trying, I quit pushing my business. On the dreary, February days, I sat looking out the window. Wanting to cry. Hating myself. Hating the world. Mad at my life. And worried that all my learning and work would amount to nothing.

I did this as CEOs and professors alike were looking at my vision sheet for my think tank and saying, "Yes! We need this! Build it!"

But I was too afraid. I binge-watched Netflix. I started looking at academic job postings again. And I lost another entire year of my life to fear.

Giving up on the dream of academia is hard. But what's equally difficult is resisting the urge to view the rest of your life through the lens of that perceived failure. For kids like me who were high achievers and did everything "right," it's a crushing blow.

Like every PhD student, I was determined to be the exception to the academic job crisis. And I became the rule.

* * *

Academia has a hold on us. For those of us who did a PhD, a career in academia is the equivalent of signing a record deal as a rock star or a hockey player being drafted into the NHL. It represents a dream of near epic proportions. Even for those who are lucky enough to build great lives outside, it doesn't mean you'll never look back. Occasionally, when you're having a difficult day, you'll put on your rose-colored glasses and yearn for those great days in academia.

The darkness, as I call it, is the space in between your lost self in academia and your new post-academic one. Having now talked to hundreds of PhDs, I can say that *almost* everyone goes through this. The darkness is the biblical valley of the shadow of death or as Inger Mewburn, author of *the Thesis Whisperer* blog, calls it: "The Valley of Shit."

For some, it's measured in time: the time between becoming lost and finding a new vision. For some, it's measured in depth: the incremental easing or worsening of feeling lost. Some come out of the darkness all at once. Some come through it in stages. It's different for everyone, but most PhDs understand what I mean by it.

February of 2019 was not the first time I'd experienced the darkness. The first, and perhaps worse, period of darkness was that one that came at the end of my PhD—the one that I started the book with. Both periods of darkness came with roughly the same emotions. The first darkness was a feeling that I would have no future in academia. The second was that I would regret leaving academia — roughly the same thing. In both cases, the darkness was sparked by fear. Fear of the unknown, fear of the future, and fear that I'd lost my one chance to make the type of impact I wanted to make on the world.

The darkness often comes when you leave academia. I don't want to pretend that it doesn't — that would be a lie. There's a time period between when you leave your PhD and when you find a career that you love. For some people it's weeks. For many more it's months. And for even more it's years. Years!

And it comes in different forms for different people. For some, it's crushing poverty, a soul-consuming symbol of your sense of worthlessness. Some PhDs get well-paying jobs, but don't feel like they're living out their sense of purpose. For them, the darkness may come despite a generous paycheck, borne out of fear of not living a life of passion and purpose

For many PhDs, the darkness is a sense of isolation and loneliness, the feeling that the people you thought cared about your future (especially a supervisor or PI) have now left you to deal with the wolves. It's the recognition that, not only do you have to walk away from what you love, but you also have to do it alone, perhaps even in the face of a department that will gaslight you and condemn your choice to — *gasp* — stop living in a cycle of systemic injustice.

We didn't talk about the darkness when I was still in academia. The reason for this lack of awareness of how goddammed hard it is to leave academia is obvious to me now: Your professors probably don't know about it. They've never had to leave. They've never had to reimagine who they are. They've never had the core of their identity shatter apart.

I was still in the darkness as I was waiting to defend my thesis. I occasionally had minor edits or a call with a committee member, but I didn't tell them what I was going through. I'd learned my lesson about talking non-academic work with anyone in my department.

My one attempt to broach the subject of non-academic work with my committee had not gone well. It had been the spring before I finished my PhD. My yearly committee meeting was a smash hit. They were impressed with my progress. We chatted for a minute about academic jobs, and I explained that I was planning to apply for some that fall. They were supportive, offering to write letters and help in any way that they could.

Then I dropped the bomb: "I'm thinking I might try to go for some non-academic jobs too."

Silence. My words hung in the air as if I had revealed that I had stage four cancer or confessed to murdering fifteen people in cold blood. My supervisor did not make eye contact. He sat quietly and seemed far too interested in the details in the drop ceiling. Finally, after what seemed like hours of silence, one of the other committee members said, "Well, we do know that that's a necessity for some students. You have to do what's right for you."

At the time, I thought that my supervisor was angry at me for thinking about leaving academia. I've thought a lot about that moment since, and I see it differently now. I wonder whether my supervisor was mad at himself for what he must have perceived to be the absolute failure of his students to get academic jobs — what he saw as the only legitimate path for a PhD.

It might be professors who hold most tightly to the myth that an academic career is the only worthwhile path for a PhD. They put their time and energy into training students for the academic job market, and they see that "important" research in their field may never see the light of day. It's a shame, then, that the source of career information for most PhD students is their supervisor.

In my academic life, I didn't know anybody who talked about non-academic work. Every student who had graduated before me was now doing a combination of crappy postdocs and adjuncting. I remember congratulating one student who graduated before me on her postdoc. She looked like she was about to burst into tears for some reason I couldn't understand.

"That will keep the wolves at bay, at least."

Since the topic of pursuing a non-academic career is so taboo, many professors never do the heavy work to understand what leaving academia actually means for students. If they did, they might understand the darkness that follows. Because most PhD students I know do not want to leave academia, and they do not turn their back on it lightly. They've wholly adopted the sense of self and identity that academia gives. They believe that the thing they are studying, whether it's grasshopper DNA or Zoroastrian rituals, is actually one of the most important things in the world. They decide that they will devote their lives to it.

Then, for a whole bunch of reasons, they can't anymore. They admit to themselves that this is futile, or that the way they're being treated is not right. The money they're making is not enough to sustain them. And they must kill their most prized possession: their tenure-track dream. The darkness is not a change of careers — it's a loss of yourself.

* * *

My academic field was religious studies. In fact, most of my life has been spent in religion. I was raised as part of an extreme, fundamentalist, dispensationalist Christian denomination that bordered on a cult. I was taught the world would be ending very soon, likely before I was old enough to get laid, which was rather depressing for a twelve-year-old. While I'm no longer particularly religious, religion continues to fascinate me as a human behavior and the study of religion permeates how I see the world.

One thing that most religions offer is a way to see the world that explains human purpose. And, as a scholar of religion, I don't only see religious behaviors in organized religion. Much of what we humans do could be characterized as *religious* behaviour: congregating, forming identities, narratives, rituals, and having ideas about purpose. You'll find this basic human behavior at any sports game, comic-con, or scrapbooking club.

Academia isn't just a neutral space; it has moral expectations baked into it. In fact, it functions a lot like a religion. It creates expectations on us and gives us identities. And it forms a sense of purpose and meaning for the people within it. In the same way as any *religion* I might study, joining academia comes with its own roles, rituals, cult-like insider language, and a *telos* — an end that we sort of agree is important (usually marked in rituals like tenure and Festschrifts).

Academics are humans. This may seem obvious, but it's worth pointing out. For all the life-of-the-mind stuff we were taught to believe and all critical thinking we did, we are still embodied creatures. We still have the muck and dirt of human existence on us and, even if we could transcend it, I don't think we should try. For this reason, leaving academia is something like leaving a religion — which I've done before. It comes with struggle, guilt, a loss of self, a loss of identity, and a fear of "what others think," but ultimately a sense of freedom.

However, I don't want to be too romantic about all this. In fact, the transformation to a life outside of academia is a very ordinary human transformation. For every human, especially those who have worked years for the same employer or in the same environment, a loss of a job is not only an economic equation. It is a loss of self and a loss of purpose.

Being overqualified, underemployed, and fearful for the future is not a PhD problem. It's a common labor-market problem. And that makes the emotions that accompany these points in time common human problems. To fear for the future is to be human. To lose your purpose and identity during a massive disruption is human.

We rarely thought critically about academic culture when I was in academia. It was easy to turn our investigative tools on other people (especially since the people I studied were dead), but it was more difficult to interrogate the structures of meaning that make up the modern academy.

For all our critical-thinking abilities as academics, we have the common human practice of sinking into the world we occupy and accepting it as if it is all that is and ever was. We act like academia simply *is* and *should be,* and rarely stop to try to understand why we construct it like this and why we expect it to go on. And, more importantly, why do we let it define us and give us our sense of purpose?

I started to wonder about this when I left. I thought about the expectation of transcendence that put us academics on a different plane from poor factory workers who lost their jobs. Most academics think they occupy a different world, a sort of noetic one that's not like the realities of other humans. We acted like we were on a different plane, set above society in the ivory tower and therefore not subjected to the human realities that hit other people.

This vanity is nothing more than delusion. At the core we are all the same, and a few extra years of education makes us talk fancier, but it doesn't take away our very-real humanness. In fact, academia is often worse than other workplaces because it refuses to be introspective, and as a result can be very toxic. I've been around a lot of companies doing the difficult work to address their shortcomings: toxic environments, poisoned leadership, bullying, racism, sexism, homophobia, etc. Academia doesn't seem as willing to have these discussions (as the hashtag #academiatoo has shown, for example) and the power of tenured professors makes it very difficult to address systemic injustice.

I've jumped in and out of enough disparate worlds over the years to recognize that each world has a structure of meaning. Each workplace, office, discipline, and field have things that they value. One of the bizarre things for me as someone who's worked dozens of different jobs, many for a short period of time, is that you come to recognize how artificial these structures are. Each is as artificial as the last, but when you step into them, the people in them take them deadly seriously. And they should. Their lives are bound up in them.

When I worked construction, there was a distinct hierarchy — not only of workers, but also of the type of work people did. Driving an excavator was one of the highest-paying and highest-status jobs, while driving a dump truck was much lower on the value scale. Being a general laborer was at the bottom.

When I got hired at the Canadian government, I noticed a similar mythology around leadership there. Employees fought to have face time with a director general or, even better, an assistant deputy minister. They wanted to work around these people of power and status. Yet this pursuit makes no sense to anyone outside of the government.

Academia is no different. For all our obsession with the status and prestige of being around celebrity profs, nobody outside knows who they are. I will occasionally see PhD students identify themselves as being "in Prof. So-and-So's lab," a distinction that doesn't make sense outside of that discipline, much less outside of academia. I've never heard of any of the celebrity professors people align with. That doesn't really matter. Once we step into this academic structure of meaning and accept it and our place in it, it forms our purpose and value too. It's important in its own way.

Whether in academia, government, a company, or a high school, humans make up these structures of meaning and exist within them. I suspect this is something like the "world creating" that Peter Berger and Thomas Luckmann talk about in their classic sociology work, *The Social Construction of Reality*.[9] Humans create worlds — it's what we do, just as we are created by our worlds. We buy into these structures and our place within them. And we promptly forget that we created them. We act as if the worlds we know are real. In fact, we may HAVE to do this for our own psychological health.

As academics, we live within these meaning structures every day. Just like every other workplace, we need to buy into them to ensure our own sanity and to believe that we are doing something worthwhile. Nobody says "tenure-track jobs are bullshit" or "my research doesn't matter" (at least nobody I know). We need to drink the Kool-Aid to function within the academic

31

structure of meaning. It creates our identity; we have a place that makes sense to us within the structure. And it gives us a clear sense of how our life will be if we keep moving up the structure.

For many disciplines, academia trains you to be an academic. While they can talk about PhD transferable skills, these skills are usually skills you gain by accident as you train for academia. The structure of meaning you're learning to exist within is academia itself. For this reason, the reinvention challenge is not simply a matter of getting a non-academic job. It's about buying into a different world. That's hard, and frankly, terrifying. I can see why people would rather adjunct, hanging out hope for a tenure-track job.

It's not about getting a job. It's about finding a new identity and leaving behind your own identity in a world that made sense. It's about work that gives us an identity. *Grad student* is an identity within academia. *Adjunct* is another type of identity — it's one of the least prestigious, but at least it makes sense in that world. So does *postdoc*.

Policy analyst does not (usually). That was my first job title when I got out. It belongs to a different structure of meaning. This structure does vitally important work too, but it does not relate to academia, but rather to a government. Reassigning myself into this structure of meaning meant buying into a whole different set of value propositions. It meant accepting a different career-progression ladder, that no longer led to *tenure-track assistant professor* but instead lead to *director of research* for a private company or a non-profit, or job working for a government department.

Transitioning to non-academic work isn't just about getting a job. It's about killing your entire structure of meaning. That hurts, a lot. And your tenured supervisor can talk a good game about non-academic work, but they've likely never had to go out and recreate their life outside of academia with a PhD. They don't know how hard it is to be in that darkness. Add to this the unwillingness of some departments to act as if non-academic careers are worthwhile and noble professions, and you have the roots of the crisis that PhD graduates leaving academia have to face, often alone.

* * *

And so, I was in the darkness. I didn't know where to go. I had no role models and no direction. But I did have a stubborn determination that I was going to figure out how to get a job with a PhD — and not just any job, a good job! Marie Forleo has a book called *Everything is Figureoutable*, and that's sort of the mantra I had. I knew that there must be a way to turn a PhD into a career, and I told myself that I would do it.

From the midst of the darkness, I had glimmers of hope that I might make it if I was determined enough. And I'm stubborn. Carolyne laughs at me because when someone tells me I won't be able to do something I usually set out to prove them wrong.

So, after the summer of darkness, I found myself at the wheel of our SUV with a 6' x12' U-Haul trailer swaying behind me, overloaded with all our worldly goods. The seven-hour drive took us out of the deep, warm summer of the woods of Northern Ontario to the hot city. As the Canadian parliament buildings and surrounding office towers came into view, I was struck by the magnitude of what I had to do.

Carolyne and I had chosen to come blind to the city of Ottawa, knowing nothing other than that there might be jobs for PhDs here. Her first language is French, so we chose a little, French community near the city to move ourselves to.

And we dared to believe that we could build a life again.

The next two months felt like a slow climb out of the darkness as I began my networking in Ottawa, meeting with everyone I could find who would talk to me. These people, strangers in fact, helped me believe that I might have a future. The first period of darkness began to lift after I started having coffees with them. Each took me very seriously as a PhD and gave me advice on where my career could go.

Nobody told me that I had to go work construction, nor did they tell me I was overqualified. I was learning the joys of being in a knowledge-economy city. PhDs are valued in Ottawa. My little gamble on starting over would pay big dividends. Because there was no better place in Canada to build a career with a PhD. Ottawa was it.

The first darkness cleared more when I got hired for my first post-academic job at the think tank. I often found myself apologizing for my PhD, trying to ensure people that even though I'd been an academic, I was a hard worker. I was answering assumptions that I felt people had about PhDs, without even knowing if these beliefs were true.

In reality, nobody thought less of me for having a PhD. They liked it. I saw the many things I could do with a PhD. I met PhDs from all walks of life doing amazing things, and the darkness completely lifted — for a while.

* * *

My department had a requirement of "professionalization seminars" that were mandatory for all PhDs. They were a new requirement that came into place the year I started my PhD. Most were to do with academic skills, but a few of them were directed towards getting jobs outside of academia. We had to do at least twelve; I recently found the notes from one that I went to in my first year and was shocked to discover that the presenter said a lot of the same things that I write on Roostervane. The advice had been there, but in the haze of my first year, I'd never considered that I might need to follow it.

I was working full-time in Ottawa. With my dissertation done and in its final stages of approval, I finally acknowledged that I needed to complete the last requirement for my degree: the professionalization seminars. I'd done some but, since I'd been traveling around the world, hadn't completed them all.

I was already working outside of academia, and I didn't want to travel from Ottawa to Toronto to get a check mark in a box. I wrote to the graduate administrator and asked if I could teach a seminar instead. When the answer came back "yes," I started preparing a session called "How to conquer Ottawa with your PhD." I focused on four streams of work that I thought were useful for people with religious studies degrees: government, think tanks, politics, and national associations. I wrote in-depth explanations of how to get jobs in each space. And I was ready.

Once the students filled the room, I told the story of how I learned what you can do with a PhD. The feedback was positive. The students were interested, perhaps a few were even excited. For some, it was the first time they'd heard a hopeful account of their post-PhD future. A couple of them asked for a website to be able to access information about non-academic careers. And with that, the idea for Roostervane was born.

I know that students need career advice. But I think that hope is even more important. There are conversations that lift the darkness just a little bit for someone in a dark place. These are the glimmers of hope that you can have a life after academia, for those who feel totally worthless and helpless. Most of us who have gone through an advanced degree have felt this at some point.

The darkness is scary, and I'm not saying it won't come back. It might. And as the Bruce Cockburn song says, sometimes "you've got to kick at the darkness until it bleeds daylight."

What can you do if you're going through the darkness?

First of all, if your darkness is linked to an actual mental health problem, get yourself some help. In fact, anyone in the darkness could benefit from a mental-health professional. Other than professionals, find people who support you unconditionally and who will walk through it beside you. The type of people who will listen without judgment but can give you some tough talk when you need it. For me, it was Carolyne. She didn't completely understand the hold academia had on me, and she was grounded enough in the real world to walk beside me through the darkness and to kick me in the ass when I needed it. And sometimes I needed it.

Second, do everything you can possibly do for yourself to take care of your mental health. I meditated, and every day I listened to things that inspired me and got me up off the couch. I tried my best to exercise to keep my mind strong, even on days when I just wanted to sit and cry. Getting your body moving helps more than you realize. Exercise. Join a class. Take a walk. Just move. Your brain is connected to your body.

These are the little things that work to pull you out of the darkness. But they treat the symptoms, not the disease. The real thing that takes you out of the darkness — I found — is hope. Sometimes hope comes in tiny moments and glimpses that you might have a great life after all, like flashes of light that come in a train window when it comes out of a tunnel and just before it disappears into another one. I had hope when I talked to people who took me seriously. I had hope when I saw job postings I could do. You need to find hope wherever you can, and perhaps one day it will be more than just a flicker — it will be a giant wave that washes over you and you're ready to live a new life.

Hope can transition to courage. Because if you can hope, you can start to dream. You can start to believe. I'll talk more about these things in later chapters, but every good thing comes from hope. It's the tiny little flashes of hope that tell you that life after just might be okay. It's the little voice inside of you that tells you that, no matter how hard things may get, you will fight until you have a great life. It's the courage to get up off the floor and start moving towards something, even though you don't know what it is yet.

And you'll rebuild your own structure of meaning. But how? You rebuild by getting around new people who speak a different language of meaning. You rebuild by learning to adapt to new realities and translating your skills to them. You rebuild by remembering who you really are, not who you are in academia. You remember the things you love to do and the things you stand for. Until one day, you'll forget about being the rock star professor. You'll realize that you don't want to be him or her – you have new role models. But what's even stranger is that you begin to forget your old self, and you're okay with it. Because you love the new one more.

4

YOU'RE NOT WORTHLESS

I n 2019, I went on the academic job market one last time. It was during the second darkness. I was already feeling worthless. I still wasn't willing to apply for terrible positions, but I decided to go for a few tenure-track jobs. It reminded me of how much I was done with academia.

The few jobs that fit me were garbage. Really. Garbage. Just reading the job postings was a reminder of how expendable I was to the committee, expected to jump through hoops for the slightest chance of their crap job: "Candidates should submit three letters of reference, a cover letter, curriculum vitae, a research statement, a teaching statement, a diversity statement, a sample course curriculum, student evaluations, all transcripts from your graduate education..." All this for a one-year position that paid $40,000 a year. I'm surprised they didn't ask for my first-born child.

Reading a job posting, even for a "good" academic job, is a perfect reminder that — in the eyes of academia — you'll always be worthless. Expendable. Your time is considered totally worthless too. Search committees feel no qualms about asking for material that takes days or weeks to develop in the hopes of being considered for the very worst possible jobs, ones that pay less than my first non-academic job did. By the way, some of these searches already know who they're going to hire. And they still ask you to spend weeks of your time getting this material together. That's how little they care about you.

After jumping through these job-application hoops, you'll get form letters that start with "Dear Applicant" instead of your name. You might have spent weeks on their application, and many can't even take the time to write your name on top of it.

As I opened my final form email from an academic job that — quite frankly — I'd forgotten I applied to, I laughed. I was glad to be free. I was working a job that already paid more than the tenure-track job I'd applied for. I was having a greater impact on humanity, working in refugee policy. The academic life had appealed to me, but it was time to be free. And I was okay with that.

So, although it felt a bit like the door was slamming shut on academia, I wasn't sorry to see it close. I was tired of feeling worthless.

* * *

Feeling worthless is the baseline condition for many PhDs, and it starts long before they enter the academic job market. Academia itself is often determined to convince you at every turn that you're worthless. It's everywhere. Academia feeds on your low self-esteem. It literally survives because you, and thousands of students like you, don't know what you're actually worth.

You come into the university feeling like you've got some great things to do, like you've got a calling. Maybe the stipend is crap, but at least you'll be saving the world. At least you'll be doing valuable research that will impact people, you tell yourself. Then, little by little, you're broken down. You're broken down by not being able to afford rent and having to live in a garbage apartment with four roommates. You're broken down by sitting at the feet of Famous Professor and realizing they don't really have the time for you or your work. You pour months into writing a chapter that takes them months to read; your supervisor is happy to take on students to do their RA work, but can't make the time to read those students' work.

Famous Professor thinks you're lucky to be sitting at their feet, when the reality is that they're lucky anyone still signs up for useless degrees to do their shitty RA work for them. They're lucky anyone still wants to study with them in the academic system that is quickly imploding.

I believe that most adjuncting is poisonous to PhD students and is reflective of the wider crisis of self-worth that doctoral programs give students. As you go through your PhD program, you get ready to take on more and more responsibility. You start to imagine that you're a leader and you step into that. But once unemployment on the academic job market hits, many PhD grads feel that they have no choice but to take on adjunct positions to weather the uncertainty, build their CV, or pay their rent. However, in doing so they become a doormat. They are totally expendable. They know it, and their departments know it.

Adjuncting is especially cruel, not only because of low pay or precarity, but because over time, adjuncts begin to imbibe the idea that they're worthless. Adjunct positions, or sessional lectureships, are when PhD students and graduates are paid on a per class basis instead of given a full academic job. They take these roles on and accept it into the core of their being, telling themselves that it's okay that they aren't full-time employees because they are great teachers and they care about their students (which they are, and they do).

Worthlessness becomes an integral part of their identity as they wait hopefully to be rewarded with the tenure-track job as it becomes available, only to see it given to someone else. Each year that goes by is an exercise in hope and heartbreak. Each cycle brings renewed expectations that, maybe this year, the university will see the hard work they've done and reward them. After all, an adjunct has built great relationships with the students, knows the faculty well, and has worked hard for the good of the department.

But the reward seldom comes. The university chases the bright, shiny object of the newly-minted, rock star PhD or postdoc who is up-and-coming in their field. The adjunct is each year surprised by how calloused and cruel the university is. But they meekly go back in line to wait for their turn that — for many — will never come. The adjunct has assented to the university's implicit assertion that they're not worthy of a full-time role. And, while it hurts, they continue working for the organization as they either adopt a martyr complex or a deep-seated rage toward the establishment, or both.

* * *

If you feel worthless, it's time to change that. Worthlessness isn't your condition. And it's not about your skill set either. Feeling worthless comes from your internal estimation of yourself. Or maybe to put it better, you feel worthless because you don't know to know how to judge yourself properly. And since the only data you have on judging your own worth comes from external information, academia dictates an academic's self-worth. Using the measurement of worth that academia gives, you consider your worth in terms of how much you know, how many grants you've won, how many peer-reviewed publications you have and, at last, what tenure-track job you've gotten. But these are terrible measures of worth.

So here it is. You are valuable, not because of what you can do, what degree you have, or what your skill set is. Self-worth is a gift you give yourself. You become valuable in your own eyes by believing that you're valuable and by constantly rejecting the inner and outer narrative that tells you you're worthless. When you let the people around you tell you what they think you're worth, and you adopt their beliefs, it's a recipe for disaster. In this world of endless competition and achievements, you can lose your sense of worth quickly.

I often hear the analogy that adjuncts would be better off working at McDonald's for the money they make. And while that's true, I also think that working at McDonald's would be better for an adjunct's self-worth. If that adjunct had gone to work at McDonald's, it would have been soul destroying — for a while. But, hopefully, they would have worked hard and learned a lot (in Canada, a stint at McDonald's now counts as a business credit in some colleges).[10] Perhaps they would have climbed the ranks to become a manager. Maybe they would have grown into executive programs. Or maybe they would have leveled up and traded their job at McDonald's for a better job somewhere else.

But do you know what would most likely happen? They would find that working at McDonald's is total crap, and they would push as hard as they could to get out! They would quit and go do something else. This tells me something too. Even working at McDonald's, a PhD might retain enough dignity and self-confidence to know when a job is beneath their skills and exploiting them — something that adjuncts often do not seem to grasp. They would be offended by the job, and they would believe that they're worth more. And because they believed it, it would be true. It would create greatness in their lives. McDonald's would make them hungry and push them to become more. They would never accept being treated as worthless by McDonald's. But they'll accept it from the university.

Now, most PhDs will not end up working at McDonald's. I use this to illustrate that even the worst-case scenario outside of academia might not be so bad for self-worth. As I explored in the last chapter, PhDs do incredible things. And they will continue to do incredible things. But those who believe that they're worthless, that they can't do anything else, have created a self-fulfilling prophecy.

Two Stories of Self-Worth

I want to tell you the tale of two adjuncts.

The first, Vincent, said to me, "It's so easy for you to say to reject adjuncting. You've got a good job. Adjuncting is all I can do. I'd love to do something else, but nobody will hire me. Find someone who will give me a good job, and I will happily quit."

The second, Erin, told me her story around the same time: "I did some adjuncting, but I knew I was better than that. I'd worked my whole life, and I knew I could find something. I quit with no plan and walked into a restaurant down the street and got a job waiting tables. It was terrible, but I kept hustling and networking and eventually met someone in marketing. I got hired by a marketing department, and a year later ended up as an assistant director of marketing for a big company!"

In these two people, I can see the stories of almost everyone I meet who wants to leave academia. Most fall into two camps. The first is made up of those who believe that this is all they're good for, or it's all that's good enough for them. They're angry that nobody will give them a job, and they tell everyone about how unfair the world is. They whine about the university, their supervisor, their students, their country, capitalism, and who knows what else. They assume that good non-academic careers are for those who are lucky or who have connections and since they believe this, they never try to build one.

The second group is made up of those who take ownership of their lives. They look at the world with their spirit of learning and say, "How hard could it be? I can figure it out." They go out and try again and again until they build the life they want. And, although they are disappointed that academia didn't work out, they determine that they are too valuable to keep being treated the way academia treats them.

There's nothing more important to your future than the things you believe about yourself. If you believe you're worthless, it's true. If you believe you have unstoppable power to do great things, it's true. I fully realize how much I sound like some cheesy motivational speaker as I write this, but I don't know any other way to say it. How is it that so many academics can talk about the "life of the mind" but do not realize how vital mindset is to success? The things in your mind will become your physical reality too.

Adjuncting has a poisonous effect on your mindset, but it's certainly not alone. Some (but certainly not all) departments are toxic cesspools of naval gazing and infighting, and — in some cases — students are worse for spending time in them. If you feel worse about yourself every time you go to a department function, this is a sign that this place is not good for your mental health. If you're having trouble getting out of a funk, or if you are a person who struggles with mental health, these environments can be poison. These are assaults on your mental well-being, but they also attack your future and your potential as they soak toxicity and negative attitudes into your core. How can you get a dissertation written in an place that kills your soul? How can you possibly write successful grant applications? And how can you build a great career?

Get around people who lift you up wherever you can find them. Get inspired and start to believe that you have greatness in you. If you don't know people who inspire you personally, watch inspirational videos on YouTube. I spend at least half an hour a day watching, reading, or listening to things that inspire me. If my success or failure depends on my attitude, then there's nothing more important than guarding that attitude. The things I believe about myself become true in my life. When I started to believe my PhD could be useful in this world, I saw it become so. My back was to the wall, my kids had to eat, and I wasn't going to have a future if I didn't push myself to create something. I had no trust funds, no savings, no connections, no powerful network.

I willed myself to create a career with a PhD. And I did. And then I started consulting and began to doubt that I was good enough to do it. This belief became true, and I failed at it. Both of these things have become self-fulfilling prophecies in my life.

One of the people that inspires me most is Oprah Winfrey. Although she's one of the most powerful people in the world, she grew up in poverty with a single mother who was a household maid. She spent time living with her grandmother, so poor that she wore dresses made from potato sacks. She faced multiple sexual abuses in her youth. At the age of fourteen, she became a single mother herself and gave birth to a child who died shortly after birth. After tumultuous high school years, she eventually would go on to create a global media empire.

Oprah's story is powerful. When I hear it, I ask myself, "What's my excuse?" So many people in this world feel sorry for themselves and can point to the many reasons they're not going to succeed or aren't succeeding. But if you have a PhD, no matter who you are, you are part of an elite few on the planet who have had the privilege of getting one. You have already done things almost nobody gets to do, regardless of where you come from.

The confidence-destroying realities of academia are terrible for allowing us to create and justify excuses. We never feel good enough and imposter syndrome waits at every turn. And when we face failure, academia rubs it in even more. We feel unworthy. Getting ignored for academic positions reaffirms our unworthiness. So, we go out into the "real world" and are told by employers that we're overqualified. After the three-, five-, seven-, ten-, or thirteen-year journey that is academia, many PhDs have no fight left.

Start from where you are to work on your mindset. Determine to be unstoppable and become convinced of your self worth, so much so that external forces won't shake it. Practice meditation, positive affirmations, visualization, or any damned thing that works to build your self-worth. Spend time around people who make you feel unstoppable, not people who tear you down. Take on your doubt and your fear. And start to believe that you're good enough.

If you raise your sense of self worth, it will help you in academia, but it will also drive you in the real world. You'll become unstoppable. Your first job might be shit. The second one might be garbage. But you will keep fighting until you live in a world that matches what you believe you're worth, and until your paycheck reflects it too.

I want to tell one final story about the battle for students' self-worth. In the third year of my PhD, the graduate student union went on strike for better pay. I watched the university administration laugh at us, dismiss us, and just generally treat us like children asking for a later bedtime. The administration told us that the university could consider adjusting teaching assistant (TA) wages, but since the stipends were not specifically in the union's realm, there was nothing they could do. And when they brought in an external arbitrator to evaluate the strike, he did exactly what the university wanted him to. They gave small concessions in the TA package but didn't address any of the fundamental inequalities that students were angry about. As you have perhaps experienced, having your TA wage raised by fifty cents an hour is not a huge lift when you only work a hundred hours a semester.

Many of the students on the picket lines were furious with the university. But, after the strike, we all went back to our carrels and our research. People spouted off angry things about neo-liberalism taking over the university, but they went back to living the lives they lived before the strike.

I learned a lot by going through the strike. Of course, I learned that the university didn't really give a shit about whether we lived or died; the institution that we were devoting our time, talents, and mental well-being to saw us as expendable. But there was a bigger lesson. Our prison was not just neo-liberalism or the corporatization of higher ed. Our prison was our own sense of worthlessness. It was the fact that we didn't know how to exist outside of the university, and we didn't have the guts to walk away. We wouldn't break up with academia, no matter how crappy of a lover it was.

We were imprisoned by the tenure track dream, of course. But in that strike, I saw what was more dangerous about when students misunderstand their own worth. By its very nature, the academic climate I knew didn't encourage students to think about non-academic careers. There was stigma about working outside of academia; you were considered a failure if you did. And therefore, the strike showed me one more outcome of being chained to the dream of being tenure-track at all costs.

Whether they meant to or not, our faculties and supervisors had built another ideological cage for us, one that made us believe that we couldn't do anything worthwhile or fulfilling outside of academia. And since they wouldn't talk about anything other than tenure-track jobs, postdocs, or adjunct positions, we didn't know that there was anything else we could possibly do. Feeling worthless was a prison. The university won the strike because they knew we wouldn't go elsewhere, no matter what they did.

* * *

So, what is the answer to worthlessness?

I can't tell you what's right for you, but I found the answer in one word: LEAVE! When I left, I began the process of rediscovering my self-worth again, although it took a while. Of course, self-worth doesn't come from a job, academic or otherwise—no matter how much we tell ourselves it will. I've had moments in my non-academic jobs where I've felt worthless too. I've never felt as taken-advantage-of as I did in academia, but I've had moments where I felt expendable.

The battle for self-worth doesn't happen on a resume or on your CV. It happens in your mind. Academia is not bad for your sense of self worth because it pays you poorly. It's bad for your self worth because it convinces you that you deserve to be paid poorly. Nobody can protect you from this but you. I sincerely hope the system changes, but you still need to build your self-worth however you can.

45

Since leaving academia, I've battled the feeling of not being good enough. In my first job, I worked my ass off and ran some great projects. But I still felt like a failure. This was partly because it was a hectic workplace, and I always seemed to be behind on what I had to do. I ran like mad to keep up with my projects. But the other, bigger reason was that I was used to feeling like a failure. I was socialized in academia to feel like what I was doing was never enough, and that I'd fall behind just by standing still.

On my last day at the workplace, my company took me out for appetizers and drinks, and my bosses took turns toasting me. They started listing things that I'd done for the company. I picked up existing projects that were disasters and ran with them to conclusion. I built relationships with key stakeholders that didn't exist before. My projects were under budget. And — in their words — I did it all with "values that shone."

I hope this doesn't sound like self-congratulatory bullshit. The point I'm trying to make is that I felt like a complete failure through my time at the company because I was used to feeling like a worthless failure. I carried that sense of myself into my first non-academic job and felt like a terrible failure there too.

When you are trained to see self-worth as something you accomplish rather than something you can always have, a sense of confusion is inevitable. Self-worth isn't from the world around. It's not something "out there" that you need to reach to feel good enough. Self-worth begins in the core of your being. You need to give yourself permission to believe that you are worthy, not because you will do great things, but you are beautiful and human. And you do have things to give.

I'm not saying you shouldn't try to achieve. I'm hella hungry, and I have a lot I want to do during my short years on this earth. But what I'm learning is that self-worth comes before success. You need to love yourself and then accomplish, not accomplish so that you can love yourself. If you do the latter, the accomplishments will seem hollow and leave you empty. If you love yourself first, the accomplishments are just a natural extension of your inner greatness, which will be there no matter what happens. Your achievements won't fulfill you, because you're already fulfilled.

5

THE LIFE OF REINVENTION

Once you face the difficulties of leaving academia and turn yourself towards building a new life, there's a new hurdle to face: reinvention. What does it take to re-create yourself as someone new? This chapter is dedicated to the painful-but-exciting process of reinvention, and I'd like to use part of my story to illustrate how it works.

I grew up in a small town in Northern Ontario in Canada. It's surrounded by hundreds of miles of what we call "bush" in every direction—forest wouldn't be an appropriate word. Tiny scrub pines and tag alders mix with the hard rock of the Canadian shield and the endless bogs of the clay belt to form it.

I was the oldest of five kids. Mom stayed home to raise us, while Dad worked as a maintenance man at the tiny local hospital. I never had a new pair of clothes, and it was a lucky day when a neighbor would bring over a garbage bag of clothes one of their sons had outgrown for me. We were poor, rural Canadians who did all we could to survive our realities.

Everyone I knew as a kid worked in either mining or forestry — there was a gold mine in every direction and a paper mill in the next town. Mill jobs were good jobs; they came with a pension and some stability. Mining jobs paid well, but miners were unemployed every four years when the price of gold dropped and the mines closed, only to be reopened a few years later when gold went up again.

As a kid, I thought it was just the way the world was. Everyone I knew dreamed of working in the mines. Every kid dreamed of taking heavy-equipment courses to either drive enormous machines or fix them. And everyone was poor. Well, almost everyone. The people we thought were rich had toys like snowmobiles and big trucks that they had either earned or financed with a mine paycheck. I wasn't interested in working in a mine, and I didn't care about who had the fastest snowmobile. And so, I didn't fit in the world I grew up in.

Like many humanities students I've met, I didn't understand my world and escaped into books instead. We had shelves full of everything from Joseph Conrad to Jane Austin to George Orwell, and I read it all. My mom had dreamed of going to university before she had me at twenty, and her connection to that dream was collecting musty books that lined walls of our house.

I swore that I would get out of my small town and see the world. I wanted to live abroad, learn languages and, most of all, do something that mattered. In my teenage brain, the generations of people who existed to work in the mines until they could retire with a pension seemed to be missing something essential about the meaning of life that I was determined to discover.

Like many poor, rural parents in Canada, mine thought that having an education would open the world for us. They thought it would give us opportunities that we wouldn't otherwise have, and certainly opportunities they didn't have. They didn't really understand the world of higher education; they'd never gone.

So, I got educated. Something interesting happened as my education progressed, something that happens to many students. I talked differently. I dressed differently. People in my hometown thought I was snobby now, especially because I was more interested in philosophy than hockey. I didn't fit anymore. I had undergone a transformation from my working-class roots that would take me years to come to grips with — an experience I now realize many first-generation students have.

And it was a serious challenge. I took pride in the fact I was from the woods, knew how to hunt and fish, and could work hard with my hands. Now that was no longer me. I felt like an imposter in the city, because I was just a simple guy from the woods, and I felt like an imposter at home, because I was the big city boy now. It was my first transition between two worlds, my first reinvention. There have been others in my life, but this was my first experience stepping out of an old reality into a new one.

* * *

My reality growing up, and the first steps beyond, marked a normal human transition. You probably went through this type of transition too. Your reality looks different, a construct of wherever you came from. But it played an integral part in forming you and your relationship to the world and leaving it to go away to school was a disruption.

In ritual theory, we called this transformation a rite of passage; it took us from one world to the next. And each of our passages between stages of life requires this type of journey. They demand that we think of ourselves in ways we never have before, and sometimes that we leave the old things behind.

There's some origin for your model of the world. If you want to reinvent yourself after a PhD, it's vital to take a good inventory of where your understanding of the world and your place in it came from. The world of academia was not my original world. I was formed into it. I spent time building my academic world and my place in it. So did you. It's important to understand that fact when it comes to reinvention. If you're going to build a different version of yourself and exist in a new world, you need to recognize that you built the first one. You get to destroy it if you want to. I'm not saying it will be easy, but it is possible.

This is what reinvention is. It's learning to value a new world and creating a new identity and structure of meaning within it. Humans do this all the time. Anyone who's ever moved to a new city or country, changed schools, or just generally overturned their social world for whatever reason has experienced this. When you're in the world of academia, it feels almost impossible to imagine yourself in any other place. We're like the kids in high school whose parents tell us we're moving to a new school. It seems unfathomable. We will scream and argue and cry. But in the end, we'll go to the new school, make new friends, and learn to love life again.

49

What does it take to reinvent yourself? How do you go through that rite of passage and come out the other side intact? This book is obviously dedicated to the whole process, but here are a few things I've learned.

Change who you spend time with

The first and most important thing is simply to change who you spend time with. Once you start to spend time with people who don't obsess about the tenure-track and your relation to it, you may be surprised to find that you begin to slip into a world you never expected to be in.

I was talking to a friend recently who started competitive mountain biking while she did her doctorate. One day, she was surprised to find that the world of academia was fading in importance; she didn't feel like she put as much stock in it. She wasn't as depressed by the future because she was finding her place in a new world as an awesome mountain biker. As she got better, her confidence grew. She learned the language of biking and found a team to be on. She now tells me she's barely even concerned about academia. Her best friends are all on her biking team and they've immersed her in a new biking world. But they also have other careers, and she's beginning to see what's possible because she hangs out with them.

Spending time with academics is guaranteed to make you believe that the sky is falling and that the world will never make sense again. When I stopped hanging around with academics, I stopped thinking like an academic. I no longer heard anything about who got tenure or who got some "prestigious" postdoc. I didn't feel like crap because other people had published and I hadn't or feel guilty because I had and they hadn't.

In fact, when I came to Ottawa, I learned the bizarre reality that stepping into a different social world completely changes your value system. I learned a whole new set of concerns, which were just as arbitrary as academic concerns: *Who's getting hired as a senior advisor to some cabinet minister? Who is appearing as a "Hill Climber" in Ottawa's political magazine, The Hill Times? What politician has a new scandal about to break? What think tank just won ten million dollars in funding to study some policy issue?*

The world is full of artificial ecosystems like this. Like I talked about earlier, these are structures of meaning. When you leave academia, you'll move into a new one and learn its language and its concerns. You may feel like an imposter there or you may love it. But at the very least, you will see that there are different ways to do this thing called life — and that's the first step to reinvention.

Stepping into a different structure of meaning has its own challenges. It's not always easy. None of these worlds are places that I inhabit perfectly, but that's okay. I got around other people who were totally invested in totally different things, and it was refreshing, even if I didn't buy their world completely. When people asked my what my PhD was in, I said, "religion and migration" and left it at that. Because that was all I needed to say. They didn't care. They were impressed that I had a PhD, but they didn't need to know the intricacies of it.

Understand the value of your story

I started this chapter with some of my story because I want to explain the most powerful thing I've learned in my time leaving academia: Our stories define us. They write our existence in ways that most people don't understand. And the thing that changes everything in your quest for a new identity after your PhD is your story: first understanding the story that's driven you to this place, and then learning how to become the author of your own story in the future.

This is a hard message to sell to PhDs who just want to know how to make a resume or how to do a job interview. But if you're in the process of leaving academia, let me tell you, DON'T IGNORE THIS INNER WORK! It's really important and will make all the difference to your career transition.

So, why stories? We human beings love to tell stories. In fact, stories are so powerful that they come to define our realities. Our ancestors sat around the fire and told stories. The stories had lessons that had everything to do from where the best places to hunt are two why you should avoid strangers.

Our society privileges stories above all else too. Have you ever wondered why movie stars are so famous? Stories become the currency of our culture, and they are so embedded in our DNA that production companies will put out hundreds of millions of dollars to tell a good story, being fairly confident they can make it back once the movie comes out. Why? Because they trust the insatiable appetite that humans have for stories.

The theory of narrative identity suggests that we create our identities through stories. We use stories to understand ourselves and the world in it. To break every academic rule I know and quote from the abstract, Dan McAdams and Kate McLean, in their work on narrative identity, write:

> The story is a selective reconstruction of the autobiographical past and a narrative anticipation of the imagined future that serves to explain, for the self and others, how the person came to be and where his or her life may be going.[11]

Narrative identity helps explain why I once imagined myself as a kid from the woods, and privileged being a hard-working, blue-collar kid from a working-class background. Like some of you, I was proud of being working class. I believed that there was something special about the blue collar, because it was where I came from. When I understood myself as a simple kid from a mining village, I felt like I didn't fit in the big city. As my own story changed away from being the person whose life revolves around hunting and mining, I began to adopt a different story about my identity that incorporated new ideas and intellectual curiosity. It also explains why I once told myself that I was an academic, wired to think big thoughts and travel the world. In my *Chris-the-academic* story, my tenure-track self was the only way I could live a life with meaning or have purpose. But that story was wrong.

Stop telling negative stories

If we tell ourselves negative stories, they keep us from moving forward in life. Some of these stories are unique to PhDs:

· I'm overqualified, nobody will hire me.

- I will only be happy as a tenure-track professor.
- If I pay my dues, academia will reward me.

These go alongside the much more human stories that everyone tells themselves, the attitudes that hold us back:

- People who make money are evil or greedy.
- I was born in the wrong place.
- People like me never succeed.

These are stories human beings tell themselves. They stick us in a rut. They perpetuate our feelings of inadequacy and drive us to embrace our worst fears, which keeps us from our greatness. Our worst stories explain why we can't have what we want.

When I hear these types of stories from PhDs — and I do a lot — I can almost instantly predict what someone's career prospects will be in the short term. People who tell themselves self-defeating, limiting stories, will have self-defeating, limited lives.

Narrative psychology talks about a phenomenon called "narrative coherence," which means that people find the evidence they need to match their story. We even do it subconsciously, as we try to keep our ideas about our own identity coherent with the world.

When a PhD tells themselves that they're overqualified, they'll focus in on people who have told them that and PhDs they know who are struggling to find work. Someone will tell me, "Managers don't like hiring PhDs," and usually this information is either based on the one manager they've ever talked to or something a friend told them. And they've never thought through how ludicrous what they're saying is.

I have to stifle a sarcastic response. *REALLY? ALL managers don't like to hire PhDs? Of the hundreds of thousands of managers in the world, none will hire PhDs?*

But this story confirms their fears and sense of inadequacy, and lets them off the hook from busting their ass to find a manager who will hire them, so they will hold on tight to that belief. It's hard to talk them out of it, because it confirms the way they want to see themselves and their place in the world.

What sort of a story do you tell about yourself? When you look at a goal that you have in your life — and I want you to picture your biggest, most audacious dream — is there a story that you tell yourself about why you can't have that? Telling yourself a negative, self-defeating story is not an academic thing. It's not a student thing. It's a human thing. But you need to cut these stories from your life if you want to move forward.

Your story is your identity. If you are in the process of changing identities, change your story. It is vital to not only identify the negative stories that hold you back, but also to begin to change your story about your own past. We can come back to narrative psychology again:

> *A strong line of research shows that when narrators derive redemptive meanings from suffering and adversity in their lives, they tend to enjoy correspondingly higher levels of psychological well-being, generativity, and other indices of successful adaptation to life.*[12]

It doesn't matter whether our stories are "true" or not. But it matters that we learn to tell positive stories about ourselves and our histories to overcome our backgrounds and begin again.

Many PhDs in the process of leaving academia need to change the stories they use to make up their identity. Sometimes, those of us who think, "I'm an academic. I'm only going to be happy as an academic," need to learn to speak a different language. In that story, you will only ever be happy as an academic, and you'll feel out of place in a non-academic workplace. Even a small shift like, "I'm a former academic," can move mountains in your life.

One of the hardest things to do is the live in a story that is at odds with the reality of your future. You just can't. It will slowly kill you. So, if you face an impossible story, it might be time to change it.

Try this. Sit down by yourself, and actually write down your story. Start at the beginning. If you want to, you could use a story structure like the "Hero's Journey" to create it. As you write your story, don't focus on the negative unless it's followed by a positive. Tell the story of your life in an empowering, productive way. You are the heroine or hero. It's your story. You get to write it.

Write it in a way that makes you feel strong and empowered. You won grants nobody else did. You got into a program that was a long shot. You moved across the country and started your life over — do you know how few people have the guts to do that? You've traveled to exotic locations. You've learned things that most people can't. In each one of those, there's not only an empowering story about the past, but also about the future. If you've learned things that not many can, you can keep learning the things you need to succeed in your life. If you've had the courage to start over once, you can do it again. Each of those moments is a clue to your drive and your abilities. They show how much you have in you. Don't sell yourself short.

Use your story to unlock your purpose... and your career

As you begin to write your story down on paper, pay attention to where you see threads that align. As a PhD perched on the edge of reinvention, you might feel that there is no consistent narrative to your life or that your story ends in failure. The truth is, the story you've been telling yourself probably isn't yours. You've been telling yourself that you're a failed tenure-track professor, someone who wasn't good enough to make the cut. You've imagined leading upper-year seminars and taking fancy research trips. That would be fun, but maybe it's not your story. You have something even better waiting for you — you just don't know what it is yet.

See if you can find threads of meaning in your story. As I looked at my life, which was made up of a lot of different jobs, I had trouble seeing any consistent narrative. But one day I realized that everything I've done has been about two things: trying to answer big questions for myself and trying to help other people explore them. It's what I did as a minister, as a teacher, as a PhD student, and as a policy analyst. That's the same thing I do now with Roostervane. My life hasn't been a series of random events; I've had the same visions and goals driving everything I do. The grand, unifying theme of my life was not a job. It was a bigger sense of calling that drove my actions.

There are strands of meaning and purpose that wind through everything you do. Whether you want to believe that these come from the universe, or God, or whether you just believe that your personality subconsciously drives you to different things, watch for those strands.

As you look at your story, find the things that have defined it. Perhaps it is a quest for knowledge. Maybe you're driven by helping people. Maybe you come alive when you feel like you discover something. Maybe you're addicted to adventure. Whatever it is, it's there, somewhere, running through the story of your life. No matter how many roles you've had, you'll find that your best roles (if you've ever felt fulfilled in work you've done) will be those that have that story running through it.

These are personal reflections, but they should give you a sense of where you need to go in your career. If you're a person who needs people, don't try to build a career in something that you'll work alone for long hours. This seems obvious, but I've seen so many people violate this rule.

So, what I want you to do is to log on to LinkedIn right now. In your "about" section, I want you to make the first sentence reflect the themes that have woven through your life's work so far, and those you'll take into the future.

Ever since I got my first junior scientist set, I've loved to discover new things.

Then, I want you to link that to something you'll do in your career.

That's why I bring a passion and sense of wonder to my research.

Finally, link it to something you could do for a future employer.

My goal is to help companies uncover something they haven't seen yet, to look at evidence in new ways, and to bring the most out of the research team.

If you do this, you'll have a tremendous career statement that links your passion to your employment goals in a way that works for both employers and you. Doing this sort of writing and thinking can help you both name your purpose and unlock different career trajectories you've never thought of.

The fundamental lesson here is that your story is also your career story. You don't need to create divisions between your purpose and your career. You can string threads between the two. This doesn't mean you'll never have to work a job you hate to pay the bills; most of us do at one point or another.

But keep coming back to this story. Keep working to fit your career into it and look for roles that help you fit your purpose.

Using your story to build the life you want

The power in exploring your story is that you begin to realize something: You are the author of your own story. Moving forward, you get to write it. Nobody else does. So many people live their lives like one giant accident, going wherever the wind takes them. Don't let that be you. Once you begin to recognize the story threads winding through your life, you can write an empowering story for your future. One of the best ways to become an author of your own story is to decide on an ending. It's hard to tell a story if you don't at least have an idea of what the ending will be. So, pick an ending or a destination, even if it's temporary. If you're in a funk right now, it sucks, but it's not how the story ends.

There's a common thread in PhDs who leave academia. Time and again, I find that one word defines how the journey goes: agency. Agency is everything, and when people don't believe they have it, they stay stuck.

You don't have to do it like me, but the thing I choose to do is to write down a list of future goals every morning. I write them in the present, as if I've already achieved them (I've heard about this strategy from a lot of personal growth experts). They help me to orient my life, and each day I write them and close my eyes and imagine that they're true.

Cheesy, you say?

Perhaps, but I've found that this practice has a tremendous effect on my mental health and the direction I give my life. They don't have to be super specific if you don't know where you're going yet.

You could write things like:

I get paid good money to help people every day.

I teach history to underprivileged kids.

I have a job that lets me engage with high-powered people.

I work from anywhere and spend most of my time with my kids.

I have discovered and patented a new treatment for Alzheimer's.

I am a software engineer for Google.

I don't get to say what your dreams are. They're yours and yours alone. But make this a practice and watch how it focuses your life. I choose to write daily or weekly goals underneath these as well.

So, if your long-term goal were, *I run multi-million dollar construction projects*, your goal for the week might be, *I'm researching and contacting three PMP certifying organizations.*

Once you visualize the end, you can start to think about how you get there. Once you can find meaning in your story, purpose, and trajectory, you become the author. And once you're the author, your life feels like it's your own again.

Push out of your comfort zone

I arrived in Berlin with my family in the fall of 2015. Berlin is a city of reinvention. I could walk in the shells of bunkers from World War II, or step into the strange world of the Cold War. I could take a short metro ride to Potsdam, a small town half an hour from the Berlin core, which has dozens of castles dotting the landscape from the Prussian nobles who used Potsdam as their playground. Today, Berlin is an international arts hub and the most vibrant city I've ever seen. It's constantly and fearlessly reinventing itself.

There were the fantastic historical museums. My daughters would come with me and we'd walk through the Ishtar gate at the Pergamon Museum or stare at creepy mummies in the basement of the Egyptian Museum. And they'd walk through the darker historical places of Berlin with us, ignorant of the sadness that had once occurred there. At three- and four-years-old, they were oblivious to it.

Every Wednesday, I had my introduction to German academia, which was a very different beast from North American academia. I had arranged through my supervisor to take part in the Lehrstuhl (seminar) of a German professor at the Theological Faculty at Humboldt University. Twelve of us would cram into a tiny office overlooking Museum Island and the famous Unter den Linden.

I tried to keep up with the discussion that was happening in my limited

German, and I quickly learned something about the German academic culture, at least in the humanities. The students were remarkably rigorous in their studying of texts and artifacts — important work for historians. I couldn't match their skills in ancient languages and ability to parse obscure Ancient Greek verbs. But they didn't privilege theory as much as the academics in North America did. Because of this, our work outputs were very different; we were products of the environments we came from. I felt out of place in an academic seminar that was the exact same discipline as mine, but in a very different context. But this discomfort made me grow.

When I was a graduate student, travel transformed me. Living in other countries changed me every time I did it, and when I stopped back in at my department in between trips abroad, I realized some people were still where I left them. They were still gossiping about the same stuff, complaining about their supervisors, bickering about who got what TA position and how unfair it was. And my world had already changed. I had been scared to go abroad. I got that nervous feeling in the pit of my stomach, and Carolyne and I had some heavy discussions about the merits of bringing our young kids to live in other places. But stepping out of our comfort zones changed us. It made us stronger. We never regretted it.

If you're about to build a life with your PhD, you'll need to step out of your comfort zone. It's not going to be easy, especially if you've never been outside of academia before. But your reinvention demands it. Your future depends on it. And you will grow more than you can ever imagine.

Ask yourself, when was the last time you were out of your comfort zone? When have you experienced the learning that comes with it? Stepping out can be terrifying but building a career with a PhD depends on it.

* * *

The world is changing so much that the only thing that's certain is that most of us will need to master the art of reinvention at some point in our lives. Our training failed to prepare us for it. We are the monks who have diligently been learning to copy manuscripts by hand right as the printing press was invented. I'm a Millennial. Many of us Millennials are a lost generation, reaching our thirties and forties having accumulated many degrees, but not having accumulated much else. A 2015 study from Deloitte found that the average American Millennial had an $8,000 net worth, a 34 percent drop from 1996.[13] The world we've been training for no longer exists, and the training isn't working for us. And the cost of entry into this old world is, ironically, skyrocketing just as the world is disappearing. Tuition costs, especially in the United States, are exorbitant and student loans are a national crisis. In fact, student debt is the U.S. government's single biggest financial asset — assuming it can collect on them. The total value of student loans dispersed is at 1.5 trillion dollars.[14]

There's more to life than net worth and financial measurements of well-being, but these numbers should still horrify us. Although I wrote in chapter one that PhDs eventually out-earn master's degree holders, an extra $10,000 a year through your forties and fifties is hardly enough to counteract the interest from $100,000 in student debt and the lost years of productivity.

You need to master reinvention to survive and thrive in this world. From the statistics, most of us aren't. But, as Berlin teaches me, reinvention is the reality of human existence. The world is always in the process of dying and rebirthing. It's been that way since the dawn of time. Every generation must reconcile with change and a world that no longer looks like their parents' one.

You will survive in this new world if you make your peace with the fact that you will need to be adaptable. Your education won't help you if you're not willing to accept this. Those PhDs who hold on to desperate hope that the old world will come back will be at the mercy of adjunct positions and a university that is more and more predatory and desperate.

Your greatest asset is that you're a learner. If you are willing to face the new reality head-on, throwing your brilliant mind at the problem of learning new worlds and adapting to them, you will be infinitely employable and valuable. If not, life will be difficult for you.

You are the answer. Your drive and creativity will help you see the world you want to see. Reinvention begins with you recognizing that the world you wished existed doesn't. Make your peace with it. Mourn the world for a while.

It's okay. I did it too. Then choose to become an expert in adapting and make the phoenix your mascot. Live a life of reinvention, and you'll never lack things to learn and do.

II

Building a Career You Love

6

FIND YOUR DEFINITION OF SUCCESS

I have a dream for PhDs. It's the thing that drives me to do Roostervane. I want PhDs to realize that they have tremendous power, and I want to see a world where PhDs are in leadership, everywhere — not just in academia. The dream was born from my own struggle with identity and career that I've written about through this book. Because of so many negative factors, I believe that too few PhDs are achieving their potential, even if they have a well-paying job.

If you're in or have finished a PhD, the challenge I want to give you is not simply to get a job. It's to go out and create the world that you want to create and the life that you want. A job, or probably multiple jobs, may well be part of that. But the goal that I envision for PhDs is bigger than simply finding jobs.

I'm more interested in how you'll create and use your own personal power and influence. This is the sweet stuff of life. Not power for the sake of power, or influence for the sake of influence, but the ability to see problems and solve them. Be a world creator and build what you want to see.

I want you to be successful.

What is success? It looks different for different people.

When I got to Ottawa, some people told me that I should get a job as a policy advisor in a cabinet minister's office or else work for the Privy Council Office, one of the Canadian government's most powerful central offices. In some ways, these jobs would be perfect for someone like me who can be a power and relationship broker, but is also quick on their feet. They need people who love people and have a bit of schmooze in them.

I've never even been tempted to take on a role in these places, despite the fact that yes, I'm good with people and like being connected to a bit of power. I can admit it.

These positions require working in downtown Ottawa for sixty hours a week, long hours overtime spent in the office with a cabinet minister finishing a policy position or checking a speech. These roles are cut-throat races to the top, and usually the ones who spend the most time in the office win.

I have three amazing little girls at home. I'm not interested in missing their childhoods. They are the most important thing to me, and I make my career decisions based on whether it fits with my kids. When I quit the government, I made a promise to them: that I would be there to drop them off at the school bus and to pick them up as often as I could.

I rarely miss.

Success means a lot of different things to different people. And too often, we chase other people's visions of it. I do this all the time. In fact, chasing other people's definition of success is pretty much the story of my life and career, and it's probably even the reason I got into the PhD in the first place. I always struggle with hearing my own voice in the noise of wanting to please and impress others. And I genuinely want to have impact with my life. This can make me vulnerable to a lot of people pleasing.

So, when it comes to high-powered jobs and being connected to politicians, I might be able to do those for a while. I'm a good policy analyst and a smart enough guy. As you probably can, I can pick up stuff and run with it, learning on the fly. But I enjoy social media marketing and design more than anything. I disappear into writing a blog post or editing a video. These are my joys. Policy and research are something I make myself do — and they are an important part of my identity. But if I didn't have the creative outlet, I'd be very sad.

One day, while I was working for the Canadian government in a nondescript glass tower downtown Ottawa, a colleague complained that she needed a graphic done for a presentation. We had some branded graphics she was trying to reproduce, and she didn't have the time for the government communications department to do it. I offered to try, with the limited government computer programs and no access to Adobe Creative Suite (my favorite set of programs in the world).

I opened PowerPoint and started making a fantastic graphic, that looked exactly like the original. Halfway through, a fellow policy analyst came and watched. She saw the smile on my face.

"What are you doing?" she asked.

I looked sheepish. "I'm designing a slide for Kate. Comms doesn't have time."

She laughed. "You actually look like you're enjoying yourself."

I thought for a minute. "I am. This is actually something I love to do."

She frowned. "Really? I always thought comms was for people who weren't smart enough to do policy."

I thought about what she said all that afternoon. Her words ate into me and made me realize that even though I had achieved what was for many people the standard of success — a high-paying government job with a pension — I was not happy. That week, I had worked on projects that made a difference and made their way to the desks on some of the most powerful people in the world.

But the only thing that really brought me joy that week was doing that slide. I was chasing someone else's version of success.

Now, before you ask, academia wasn't really the thing that made me happy either. In fact, most of my life I've struggled with feeling worthless, wanting respect, not smart enough, and not capable enough. If I'm honest, I've often hated what I've seen when I looked in the mirror. I never learned to love myself, and because of that I'd hoped that first a PhD and then a great career would earn me respect and love of people. They didn't. I still ended up unhappy and lost, searching for a life that brought me meaning.

I'm an oldest child with serious self-esteem issues. I care way too much what people think about me. And a side effect of this has always been doing work that is seen as impressive by those around me. I want to be respected. I can name drop with the best of them, and I really loved how people "oohed" and "ahhed" when I told them that I was traveling to some conference in Italy or doing a research fellowship in Germany. It sounded damned impressive. But they didn't change the fact that I felt inadequate, an imposter in every area of life that was about to be found out.

It took me most of my life to discover this most dangerous part of my personality. I have such a need to do work that impresses other people that I will do things that make me miserable. I hate it, but it's the way I'm wired.

I chased status and respect for too long.

In my spare time, I was writing blog posts for Roostervane, disappearing into the language and the stories. I loved getting lost in writing, perhaps one of the things I liked most about academia too. But this felt even more powerful. My writing was impacting people. I'd cry happy tears when someone sent me a message saying that my work had been helpful to them, and I knew my little voice was making a difference in the world. Something I loved doing actually fit with something the marketplace needed — and I knew somehow this would be a part of my future.

* * *

In the closing of his book *What Color Is Your Parachute?*, Richard Bolles writes that sometimes you have to ignore the map written on your resume or CV and follow the map written on your soul. For some PhDs, following this map means that success will only mean a tenure-track job and nothing else, and they'll fight until they get it. But if we were honest with ourselves, many, like me, come to realize that they were chasing that tenure-track job for reasons that are not healthy or proper. Or we realize that academia would be a great life if we could get it, but we're not going to. And we give ourselves permission to stop believing that this is the only thing that could ever make us happy, and we go out into the world to see if there's something else that will.

I'm not particularly religious. If you asked me — a very serious academic who studied religion as an anthropological and sociological discipline — whether destiny or fate is real, I would probably get tongue tied. How the fuck should I know?

But whether you believe that it's God, or the universe, or whatever directs you towards your calling, or whether you just instinctively know that sometimes humans end up where they never expected to be, there's a beauty in turning your plan B into plan A. The tenure-track job seemed like a great idea, and perhaps it would have been a good life. But too many PhDs are tempted to see not getting a tenure-track job as a sign to tame their dreams. They shrink their huge ambitions, like a turtle pulling its head into its shell, and stop dreaming — or make their dreams very small.

If you were only to take one lesson from this book, let it be this: Don't shrink your dreams. Failure doesn't mean you're dreaming too big, and it isn't a chance to stop imagining a great life for yourself. Instead of making your dreams smaller, why not make them bigger? Why not expand them rather than shrink them? And—this is vitally important—why not take a really hard look at the things that made up your dreams in the first place? Ask yourself why you wanted those things, and whether there's a different way to get them.

Why did I want to be a professor? Truth be told, I wanted to travel around the world. It's what I've always wanted. I have a wanderer's soul. When I was seventeen, I played in a heavy metal band and I wanted to tour the world, living in the back of a van with seven other sweaty, smelly teenage dudes. It never (really) happened, although we did a few very small "tours."

My desire to have adventures was at the heart of this dream, not making music. I'm the small-town kid raised in the woods in Northern Canada who always saw the outside world as some untouchable — yet exciting — place. I always dreamed about seeing a world beyond my tiny town of loggers and miners. I knew there had to be something bigger. I desperately wanted to explore. But, until my honeymoon, I'd never been on a plane.

When I met my supervisor, he flitted off to Israel, New York, or Belgium every other week for an important conference. I'd see him on a Thursday and then again on the next Tuesday, and in that time, he'd been to Paris and spent some time in the Louvre. I thought I had found my calling. It was my dream come true.

I enjoyed the work and the research. But I loved the travel. That was what prompted me to do the schoolwork I did. And it's actually one of the reasons

I don't regret my PhD. Because although I never lived the jet-setting life of my supervisor, I still lived in France, Greece, and Germany. I felt like James-Fucking-Bond when I woke up in a new country or conversed in a new language. Yup, I lived a charmed life.

One day, I realized that I'd taken from the PhD exactly what I wanted: adventure. I'd followed the map written on my soul. My time in academia wasn't a failure. It gave me exactly what I wanted, and therefore it was a resounding success. And I decided that adventure was the thing I'd be chasing with the rest of my life, even if I wasn't chasing tenure.

What about you? What does your internal voice tell you? What is pushing you towards your dream? Do you stop to think about it?

Maybe for you, success is being the first in your family to earn a degree, as I was. Maybe success is the ability to teach and shape young minds. Maybe success is having the money to travel and never come back, or maybe you want the freedom to stay home and never leave. Maybe you want a woodshop or a garden. Maybe you really want more time with your kids, your partner, or your pet, or maybe you want a big important job that keeps you crazy busy and pays you big bucks. Maybe you need to be doing something that's saving the world, perhaps literally saving lives. Maybe you need to be preserving and valuing things nobody else cares about.

I don't care what it is you want. There's something that is driving you and that brought you to academia in the first place. You had something to gain or something to prove. You wanted to discover things or you wanted to have your mind opened. Almost none of these things are exclusive to academia. In fact, many of these goals might be better pursued outside.

Take the time to look deep inside yourself, into the part of you that was once called the soul. Analyze yourself and try to figure out what drives you. Are you being driven by your healthy dreams or by your poisonous fears of inadequacy? Is your life on autopilot, or are you still driving?

These are important things to ask.

How to find your definition of success

If you're ready to redefine what success means to you, try this. Sit down with a piece of paper today and write down some things that success means for you. YOU, mind you. Not other people. If it's helpful, you can even write a list of things you are doing to appear successful for other people that are NOT EVEN THINGS YOU WANT. I've been there. I see you.

Get specific about what you want and why you want it. Then try to identify a career goal that connects to what you want.

Here's my list:

1. I want to spend as much time with my kids as possible. Functionally, this means picking them up off the school bus, reading them stories every night, and going on adventures with them. This is my definition of success as a dad. **Career Goal — Flexibility**

2. I want to be a writer and speaker who radically reshapes the way we think about education and who teaches people how to build amazing lives with the degrees they have. This probably means interacting with government and policy leaders on a regular basis to drive better education policies forward. But more specifically, it means becoming a thought leader who speaks to people around the world and helps them build amazing lives. I want my writings to reach millions of people. Why? Because helping people through my writing makes me come alive, and because I felt there was no one to help me turn my degree into a career. **Career Goal — Impact**

3. I want to be a world explorer, living in different countries and learning as many languages as I can. I've lived in Greece, Germany, and France (and speak those languages). I want to live in another country once again with my family. These family adventures have been the best part of life. **Career Goal — Adventure**

4. I want to build a house for my family that's not too big, but that's in the woods somewhere. I was raised with access to the wilderness, and I miss it. This is for my soul. **Career Goal — Inspiration**

These are just a few of my many goals. But look at the words I've written next to them. Each of these career goals represents things that I once thought academia would give me. I was attracted to academia because of the **flexibility.** I loved being able to work mostly from home and to come to the university when necessary. I imagined doing this for life and only coming in to teach courses and hold office hours. I was also attracted by the **impact.** I felt like having top publications in my field and doing great work would have given me a sense of impact that I craved and leave something for posterity. I thought academia would give me **adventure,** as I used research grants to jet off to libraries and archaeological sites around the world. And I wanted to be in places that **inspire** me.

If I'm honest, these are the things I've been chasing my whole life. They are the values that led me to wanting to be a musician playing in a band. They brought me into academia. And at the end of the darkness, as hope begins to dawn again, there they are again. They've never left me, and my desire to achieve them has never had to diminish.

There's no plan B. I'm still chasing the things that were plan A all along. I just didn't know what they were. I thought a tenure-track professor job was going to give these to me, but I'm finding them another way. And now that I've started my own company, I'm discovering all of the **flexibility, impact, adventure**, and **inspiration** that comes with entrepreneurship.

These things drove me, and I could feel my life out of sync when I didn't have these in a row. For example:

- Working for the government gave me **impact**. I worked with important people on important issues, and I could chase that. But I had to be in an office all day and didn't see my kids.
- Being in academia gave me **adventure**. I flew around the world and lived in different places. But at the end, I felt I wasn't having impact anymore and I didn't feel that I'd be inspired by a life as an adjunct.

Whatever your goals are, take the time to get down on paper what you want and why you want it. Be as specific as possible. Why do you want the tenure-track job? Is it because you want to be significant? Do you crave discovering new things? Are you hoping to be a trailblazer as someone who is underrepresented in your field? Or are you excited about teaching and want to pass along knowledge to the next generation?

Then look at the list you've created. Is academia the only way to get those things? Is a tenure-track job the only way to achieve those goals? (It almost never is.)

- You want to do something significant? Maybe you'll end up running a non-profit that changes the world.
- You want to discover new things? Maybe you'll be a scientist working for a huge company and get paid big bucks to do it.
- You want to be a trailblazer in a field in which your identity is underrepresented? There are a lot of places that need better representation. Maybe you're destined to be a powerful voice in media instead of academia. Or maybe it's finance or politics.
- You love to teach? Maybe you'll teach high school or community college instead of at a university — a calling that's just as noble. Perhaps you'll teach executives how to write or lead cultural sensitivity courses with big companies.

Behind your drive and path into academia are ideals that you are chasing and leaving academia doesn't necessarily mean giving those up. It might just mean finding them in other places.

The words "plan B" and "AltAc" are commonly used to describe non-academic careers. I occasionally see people upset about the use of these words, as if they're stigmatizing non-academic careers. The more I meet PhDs doing amazing things outside of academia, the less I care about the apparent "stigma" of leaving academia. The further out I get, the less it matters.

In fact, as soon as you get around amazing PhDs who are doing awesome things outside of the academy, you won't care in the least about not "making it" in academic terms. You'll look back and wonder why so many people can't get out of the academic trap. Why do so many think it's the only way to live a meaningful life?

* * *

After a few months of blogging at Roostervane, something strange began to happen. I was getting notes and questions from students. But I also began to get messages from tenure-track professors. They confessed to being a variety of things: miserable, overworked, underpaid, unfulfilled. They talked of wanting to leave academia.

I couldn't believe it. They had THE DREAM! Students were all fighting as hard as they could to get to this dream of the tenure-track job, and people on the other side were telling me how unhappy and unfulfilled they were. (Although, of course, many tenure-track and tenured professors love what they do!)

A friend of mine tells the story of leaving a tenure-track history position. She spent her whole academic career fighting to get into the position she was in, and then was disappointed with what she found. She found herself teaching the same four classes every year, knowing that all she had to do was keep going at the bare minimum and she'd get tenure. There was nothing to fight for. The mad rush of the PhD and the excitement of getting a position faded into predictability and, as she tells it, boredom. To make matters worse, she was facing the infamous two-body problem, with an academic partner in a different city. Paying for living in two different places made the advantage of dual incomes virtually non-existent.

She quit and now runs a tech startup.

Dreams are important, and there's nothing wrong with dreaming of a tenure-track job. But we can only dream of what we know. Our dreams, and by extension, our definition of success, are shaped by the way we understand the world and our place in it. I never dreamed of running my own company until I worked for a few different ones and said to myself, "I think I can do this better."

The more we learn about the world, the better we'll dream, and the more arenas we'll have to live out our version of success. If you think a tenure-track job is the pinnacle of human achievement, that's what you'll dream about. But once you start to get around some people who are doing very different but just as impactful things, this may change. Figure out what success means to you in broad strokes and start chasing it. You never know where you'll end up.

7

LEADERSHIP

I f there were a skill I'd say more academics need, it's leadership: the leadership of one's own life and by extension, leadership that spills over into the world around us. We need more academic leaders who can step into the non-academic world and transform it.

Two conversations have driven home for me the difference between a leadership mindset and a follower mindset.

One day, at a conference around the middle of my PhD, I was talking to a grad student about his research. He was approaching his sixth year in the PhD and had never published anything. He was bemoaning the fact that his supervisor had not asked him to publish anything.

"She knows my work. She'll read it and tell me it's good. But she never tells my to publish it."

I was confused. I'd published several things by this point. It never occurred to me to ask my supervisor if I could or should. I'd just done it.

"Are we supposed to wait to be told to publish?" I asked.

He shrugged. "I dunno. I figured if she liked it, she'd tell me."

"Have you ever told her you'd like to publish something? And perhaps asked her how to get there?"

He looked at me for a minute and finally shrugged. "I guess I never thought of that."

Although he knew what he wanted, he hadn't taken the steps to make it happen. He'd been passively waiting for someone else to give him permission to build his own career, and in the meantime had been making all sorts of negative assumptions about the supervisor and her view of his work.

The second conversation went differently. In late 2019, I was having coffee with a founder of a clean energy startup. The company was doing well, and she was excited about the future.

"What made you decide to start the company?" I asked.

She shrugged. "It drove me up the wall that nobody was really doing this well, so I wanted to create something."

That's it! That's what so many students are missing! In that little statement is the single expression of the world creator that I talked about earlier. She saw what she wanted, and she decided to build it.

She didn't need permission. She didn't wait for it. She made the decision about what the world needed and decided to bring it into existence.

Academic institutions like to throw around the word leadership. They'll use slogans like, "training leaders of tomorrow." But few of them give serious thought to training leaders. In fact, they often seem to take away the leadership skills students had when they entered. Some of the best leaders I know had little or no formal university training, while many of the most educated among us sit around waiting for permission to do things.

Students who are waiting for their professor's permission to be great will sometimes wait for a long time, especially when it comes to building a good life outside of academia. Your PI or supervisor may not be one of the ones that's going to tell you to go and look outside of academia for a job. Some never do. If you are waiting for them to say it, you might wait for years. A supervisor is not a parent, and they won't be there to hold a grad student's hand when they're collecting food stamps after their fourth postdoc.

Make the decision to do what's in your own best interests. Run your own life. Too many of us are grown-ass adults sitting around, waiting for a supervisor with god-like power to tell us how to live our lives and what do to about our futures. It's mind-bending to me that I was going to move to any damned city on God's green Earth that gave me an academic job. I desperately wanted to live in the south of France. But I was going to spend the rest of my life in

Regina because there was a job there? Do you know how messed up this is? Even the most indecisive of the people I know at least have a say in what city they live in. Academics don't even get this.

What if more of us became decision-makers instead? What if we exercised agency in our lives and career and, like my second friend, decided what we want to build in this world? Stop and realize how many people in this world don't direct their lives. They wait for something to open up and adjust their life accordingly. I'm guilty of this. A life on autopilot is what most people go for, but a life where you decide what you want and go for it — that's the sweet spot.

* * *

I sort of secretly love the book *Rich Dad Poor Dad* by Robert Kiyosaki. He's got a lot of controversial wisdom about wealth, but one of the most interesting observations is that the school system was not created to teach people how to create their own world, business, or wealth. Most of the education system operates under Industrial Revolution principles that are meant to produce employees. It's meant to create cogs in a machine. It's easy to produce people in boxes called Doctor, Lawyer, or Engineer. It's endlessly reproducible; there's an agreed upon sphere of knowledge and expertise. But the most interesting take-away for me from this observation is that education is not made to create leaders; it's made to create followers who are worker bees and rely on someone else for a paycheck. It makes people to fit in the boxes while the world continually rewards those who think outside of them.

Seth Godin talks about this phenomenon too in his book *Linchpin: Are You Indispensable?* He says that while we are trained to fit into these boxes, our society paradoxically rewards those who step outside the box and become memorable. Although we are trained to be interchangeable, our world rewards the unique, creative, problem solvers.

Perhaps this is why the best lessons I've learned about careers have come from entrepreneurs. They showed me what it was to imagine something and make it happen — to create the thing in the world that you think needs to be there. Academia taught me to complain, to be a victim, to wait for permission, and to question everything about myself. It taught me to wait for others to solve my problems instead of fixing them myself.

It's interesting to me that many of the people I learned leadership from were not in higher ed. I always wondered why some of the people who take on leadership most readily are those who have not studied much (notice I'm not saying anything about how *effective* that leadership is). It's difficult for students used to working for a proxy boss (i.e., a PI or supervisor) to find their leadership voice at all, a particular deficiency when PhDs who succeed in the world outside of academia are often expected to be leaders.

The story of the grad student and the entrepreneur doesn't highlight a difference in skills, but rather a difference in *attitude.* The grad student said, "I can't do this without permission or someone else's opinion." The entrepreneur said, "I *have* to do this. Nobody else is going to do it." They also say, "Nobody is going to do it for me."

It might seem a little silly to compare a grad student and an entrepreneur. But I've been both, and I've learned a lot about the nature of work and education from each role. The grad student waits for permission. The entrepreneur acts or they starve. There are contrasting emotions and attitudes reflected in this difference. The willingness to take ownership is important. So are expectations around work. But without a doubt, taking action is the main difference.

There's another factor too: confidence. The worst legacy of academia for grad student identities is that it crushes our confidence. We learned that everything we said was probably wrong and should be qualified with a footnote, lest someone fixate on a minor word that we used or question our methodological assumptions.

As you may notice from Roostervane, I'm working hard to destroy these tendencies and just say what I want to say. But what you don't see is the constant anxiety about sharing my opinion that still haunts me and the imposter syndrome that I feel everyday about talking about non-academic careers, especially when someone disagrees with me.

Entrepreneurs face high levels of imposter syndrome, just like academics.

But most of them go out and deliver something anyway. They put something into the marketplace even though they're scared. They make a decision. They take an action. From actions, they have successes that grow their confidence. The confidence they grow allows them to make the next decision more easily. So begins a beautiful cycle of growing your decision-making capabilities.

Leaving academia and having some semblance of "success" when I thought I was going to be a big failure was one of the biggest confidence boosters in my life. It was the attitude that I could learn to do something meaningful with my degree that made all the difference. Every grad student can and should adopt the spirit that makes them willing to strike into the world, know what they want, and chase it. Many of us will work for companies. And if you can step into a business as someone who's willing to make decisions and act on them, you'll be a tremendous asset in a world of people waiting for instructions or permission. You probably won't get this skill from your education. Go make decisions as if your career depends on it. Because it might.

PhDs who are looking for an employer to tell them what to do, validate them at every step, and hold their hand will be totally expendable. PhDs who can see the big picture of an organization and make decisions in the company's best interest (within reason — I'm not saying to be a complete maverick) will always stand out. PhDs who can take the ownership to learn new things in an organization will be tremendously valuable.

It's hard to instantly transition into being the kind of person who makes decisions naturally. It's nearly impossible to go from crushed, defeated graduate student to confidence overnight. It just isn't going to happen.

There are probably a few answers to this. But here are two basics:

Internalize that you need to make decisions to take control of your life

This is half the battle. If you want to take control of your life, you need to start accepting your role as a decision-maker before you'll be able to make any decisions. Look yourself in the mirror every morning and say, "I make decisions" to yourself like you mean it (I know it's cheesy, but try it!).

Look at your world. Every day you have a chance to be a decision-maker. Every day we put choices off. I put off decision-making all the time, waiting for other people to make them for me or for options to disappear with my inaction. When we talk about "doors opening" and "doors closing," it's too often an excuse not to make a decision and chase what we want.

You're a decision-maker.

Tell yourself this.

Find ways to make them

We are faced with hundreds of decisions every day, many of which we make without thinking about them. Some of them we put off making for days, weeks, and years. Once you've internalized that to be a leader means to make a decision, start to make them.

Recognize that indecision is the enemy of success.

Choose, no DECIDE, to adopt an entrepreneurial spirit about your own career. Just like my friend and his publishing dilemma, there are PhDs waiting to be told whether they can look for jobs and which jobs they can apply for. Even more disastrous, there are PhDs who know they should leave academia, but are waiting for the stars to align or for someone to give them permission. For many of us, it's never gonna happen. Your supervisor might never say, "Yeah, this isn't working out. Maybe you should take a shot at non-academic jobs instead."

You are the CEO of your career. I've heard a few people say this, and it's completely true. Nobody cares about what's best for you like you do. If you can make a decision about what you want and where you're going, you're off to a good start. Here are some decisions you can make:

1. Decide how you deserve to be treated.
2. Decide how much you're worth.
3. Decide to take a chance on yourself.
4. Decide to meet some people working outside of academia to see if anyone is doing something interesting.
5. Decide on a date when you'll leave academia if you haven't found a tenure-track job.

* * *

I've jammed two parts of leadership together in this chapter: leadership in your life and leadership in your career. The two are closely connected and the first leads into the second. When you become a decision-maker in your own life, it allows you to become a leader in society. It builds your confidence. It gives you direction.

PhDs need to be leaders. First of all, this is because it's the only way to truly get paid what you are worth for your level of education. Secondly, with the critical thinking skills you've developed during your PhD, you have some natural, raw qualities that leaders have. They just need to be developed a bit.

So what is a leader?

Just as with leadership in your own life, in the "real world" a leader makes decisions.

Everyone else hides behind superiors and indecision.

If leaders make the wrong decision, they own up to it and take responsibility. But the next time, they'll still make a decision again.

If you want to be a leader, you'll have a lifetime of making decisions. You won't get them all right, but that's okay. Like being a decision-maker in your own life, leadership in the world is something you can practice and nurture.

Some PhDs are natural leaders, a gift that serves them well outside of academia. Some, like me, are just wired to do what needs to be done. When everyone in a group is looking at each other thinking, "someone's got to take charge here," I almost always will step up. If you're reading this and do this too, I see you. We even promise ourselves sometimes that we won't be such keeners, but that hand inevitably creeps up. We inevitably step up to lead if it's needed.

For those of you not wired like this, I get it. You hate us. At the very least, have some compassion on us poor souls who suffer from *volunteeritis*. You might chalk this need up to our psychological wiring — and maybe you'd be right. Some people are just like this. I've found oldest children often are the type of people who step up and take charge, especially when given instructions by an adult. There are even some studies that suggest that this is a trait of eldest kids, but as far as I can tell these are not conclusive.[15]

I meet a lot of PhDs in high places who are natural leaders. Although people often think of PhDs as shy recluses, I have not found this to be the case. Many PhDs seem to function very well in leadership. And even if they're not naturally extroverts, many can learn to grab attention and lead the show if necessary.

Why do I say natural leadership is a gift for PhDs? Because — and I'm sorry to say this — I really do believe that we need to become leaders to thrive in non-academic work. Those who do not have leadership abilities by nature or by nurture will have to work hard to develop them. Despite the fact that some PhDs can do fine jumping into certain jobs and disappearing, many of us will need leadership skills to survive — and here I'm specifically thinking about career-oriented leadership skills.

Why do I say this?

Quite simply, you're too educated not to be a leader. Society has certain expectations of people who walk around with letters after their name. When your medical doctor comes in the room, you want them to be confident and take charge. You don't want them to shyly sit in the corner or to respond to your questions with, "I don't know. What do you think?" You want them to tell you what to do! It's the same with a lawyer. If you hired a lawyer to help you with a speeding ticket, you would want them to take charge and tell you what to do!

As PhDs, we can't boldly take charge in every situation we encounter in the workplace, but we can learn to confidently state an opinion (and, of course, to have the humility to admit when we're wrong). We can learn to present something in an engaging way. After all, isn't that what we did in academia? We can dress well and carry ourselves in a way that says we're people who deserve to be taken seriously. We can know that we're worth more than basic entry-level jobs.

Yet these are things that PhDs struggle with all the time. So many PhDs come to a job interview like poor, begging, Oliver Twists, pleading with the almighty job-giver for some table scraps from the corporate world. And the employer sees someone who's studied for fifteen years and can't even look them in the eye. The PhD would do so much better if they went into interviews confidently, thinking, "I'd be a great catch! I wonder if this job will be good enough for me."

Academia doesn't seem to *produce* leaders. We've talked in previous chapters about how it zaps confidence, destroys your sense of worth, and leaves you waiting for permission to sneeze. So, it may not be a surprise that under these conditions, students don't come out as confident leaders who are willing to step up and make decisions — either in a job or about their own life.

Yet it is those leadership skills that will make a critical difference in your journey into the "real world." Leadership — especially when combined with intelligence, domain knowledge, critical thinking, and training — makes you a tour de force. All the rest of these skills without leadership will get you a lifetime of sitting around, waiting to be told what to do by someone with half your education.

Resources for developing leadership skills

Books

LinchPin: Are You Indispensable?, Seth Godin

I mentioned it above, but *LinchPin* is a fascinating book that explains why it's so valuable to be creative and memorable. It's a great read for everyone trying to build their leadership flame and helped me embrace my original voice.

Daring Greatly: How the Courage to Be Vulnerable Transforms the Way We Live, Love, Parent, and Lead, Brené Brown.

While this doesn't immediately seem like a leadership book, I love Brené Brown's work on vulnerability. It's vital stuff for building leaders too, because good leaders form the most meaningful connections by being vulnerable.

Steal the Show: From Speeches to Job Interviews to Deal-Closing Pitches, How to Guarantee a Standing Ovation for All the Performances in Your Life, Michael Port

I mentioned this book on the Roostervane blog a while back. Michael Port is a former actor who argues that we all play different roles in our lives; it's a normal human process. Moreover, we can develop our character (i.e., as a leader) and "play" that part.

The Confidence Code: The Science and Art of Self-Assurance — What Women Should Know, Katty Kay and Claire Shipman

Societal expectations of leadership interact with our constructions of gender roles. This book identifies the way that these expectations hold women back, but also offers some powerful lessons for helping women grow their confidence. I've had it recommended by several female leaders I respect, and I found the book to be a useful challenge to the gendered construction of workplace dynamics.

Podcasts

Without Fail

A podcast dedicated to success and failure, telling the stories of how they affect us.

The Entreleadership Podcast

Interviews with some of the top entrepreneurs in the world on life and leadership.

YouTube

Impact Theory and *Women of Impact*

These two YouTube shows, hosted by Lisa and Tom Bilyeu, who were founders in Quest Nutrition, interview some of the greatest leaders from all different spectra of human life. They are both must-watch shows for those learning to be leaders.

* * *

Stepping into leadership does not mean that you'll be the boss of every job you get. I'm not saying you'll never make mistakes and I'm not saying to arrogantly flaunt your PhD to everyone around. That's a great way to alienate people. But I am saying that you should find ways to be a leader — remember, leaders make decisions — in whatever you do! This might mean going to the boss and saying, "We're spending all our time doing X thing. I don't think it's efficient and I think we could do it better." It might mean speaking up in a meeting. By the way, it might also mean having the self-confidence to know when to shut up and work with someone else's idea.

You're too educated not to be a leader! If you're wired like me, that gives you a bit of a boost. If you're a shy introvert struggling with anxiety, that might be enough to provoke a panic attack. But whatever way you want to read it, if you nurture and develop your leadership skills, you will live your best life.

You're never going to be a perfect leader. Nobody is. But if you work at it, you can become a good leader. I've worked enough in the non-academic world to have seen a lot of bad leaders. They're there too, just like in academia. Bad leaders micromanage. Bad leaders let their own issues, inadequacies, and insecurities get in the way of helping their people to succeed. They yell and blame. They harass and belittle. Or, they are so passive that they might as well not be leaders at all. I've seen all this.

You'll probably work for a few bad leaders during your career. Instead of blaming them or whining about them, use them as an inspiration to push you forward in developing your own leadership flame. In every organization I've worked for, I've looked at the leadership and thought to myself, *I can do better!* (Now that I'm actually leading my company, I realize that it wasn't as easy as I thought, but that's a different story!) Learn the art of leadership and make it a lifelong study. You'll be on your way to having a fulfilling career and being paid what you're worth.

Do you know what the beauty of recognizing yourself as a leader is? When you mix leadership abilities with your world-creating power that I talked about in chapter two, you'll find that you can build whatever you want in this world. It will take a lot of work, and you don't get a free ride, but just watch what you'll do. The results will surprise you!

The world needs you. And yes, it needs your leadership skills. If you can transform yourself into a PhD leader, you will be rewarded with influence, complexity, impact, and often wealth too. Wrap your head around this. Stop asking permission. Don't even ask forgiveness — you're not doing anything wrong by being a leader. Do what you need to do to protect your well-being and launch your career. After all, you're not on a journey to getting a job. You're on a journey to building the life you want to live and the world you want to live it in. And that's a million times better.

8

NETWORKING

The man sitting in front of me looked like a used car salesman. He talked fast and shook hands firmly. I was sitting in a plush chair looking out over the parking lot of a strip mall in Ottawa. This was the branch office of one of the realtors in town. Jim was a slick operator, and I was in his world.

This was my first sort-of post-PhD job interview. To be a realtor — selling houses.

"Chris, what is your personal network?" he asked, leaning a little too close to me for comfort.

I looked blankly at him, not sure what he was asking.

He went on. "How many people do you have in your personal network? That you could personally call today if you had to, and they would know you and take the call?"

"In Ottawa?"

He nodded.

I searched the depths of my mind for a reasonable answer that was going to get this guy to take a chance on me as a realtor. I'd been in the city for one week. I could count on one hand the people I knew.

"About 100?" I lied, trying my best to look him in the eye.

He smiled. That answer seemed to satisfy him. He promised that I was in good hands with him. He was uniquely qualified to turn me into a great realtor, and he pointed to the plaques on the wall behind him signifying his sales achievements, listing values as he rhymed them off one by one.

"One hundred thousand, two hundred thousand, five, one million."

I made myself smile as I shook his hand. Then I left, realizing that I was not going to be a realtor.

* * *

I didn't know it at the time, but the question that seemed so gross coming from a slick salesman would come to be the defining question of my career. It's also the question I ask PhDs again and again. *What's your personal network?* Everyone needs one.

I hear people complaining about networks sometimes. They are upset because they assume a personal network is some illustrious thing reserved for the uber successful. Some people throw around words like "privilege" when describing people who have a strong network, assuming its some sort of Vanderbiltian status that launches the careers of the successful through contacts forged at daddy's hedge fund or mother's book club.

The reality couldn't be more different. Most of the people I meet are not blessed with such networks. They build their network one coffee at a time. One connection at a time. They face a lot of rejection, but they talk to anyone they can. And then, just like writing a dissertation, they wake up one day and realize how far they've come. Meanwhile, the complainers are still sitting at home, whining that the people who are getting opportunities are lucky in a way that they're not. They could have used the time to build a great network, but instead, they complained and used their assumptions as an excuse for inaction.

Let me tell you what I learned from Jim (the realtor) about how PhDs build amazing careers. Jim told me that he uses software that plows through his thousands of contacts and spits out ten to fifteen names a day that he calls. He remembers their kids' names (with the help of the software). He drops by with poinsettias at Christmas. Jim works his ass off to build relationships with his clients so that when they sell a house or know someone who wants to, he'll be at the front of their minds. Jim takes his network seriously.

The single greatest asset you have in a job hunt is a network. I started building mine when I came to Ottawa. Now, there's no way in hell I'm cold calling fifteen people a day, and I'm sure not dropping by people's houses. But I did learn from Jim that a network is an asset and should be treated as such. It's something you grow.

Be intentional about your network. That cheesy old saying, "Your network is your net worth" is not wrong. This applies to the quality of your network, of course. You will find jobs and opportunities open up based on the people you know and your reputation. The more you do good work and grow your network, the more opportunities you will find come to you. Often the first few contacts, just like the first job out of the PhD, is the hardest. Once you have a few contacts, they will introduce you to other people. Before you know it, your network will snowball.

* * *

One morning I was having a conversation with my spouse about this chapter, and she expressed something that everyone says:

"I hate networking." But then she continued, "At least, I thought I did... But when I went to that women-in-design networking event, it was amazing! It was a group of us sitting around and listening to senior and successful people talk about design." (She's a graphic designer.) "They told us that they would happily meet with any of us young designers if we wanted advice."

She had gone to this career event for female creatives a few months earlier. A few weeks later, she went for two separate coffee talks with two of the women she met at that event; both are senior designers in their fields.

"It felt so natural. We just had great conversations about everything from our work to the kids. I came away energized and excited for the next steps on this project I'm working on!"

THAT'S NETWORKING!

Most people have an expectation about networking that's nothing like the reality. When I tell people to network, people usually respond with disgust.

They'll say something like, "I want to network, but it's not my style. I hate schmoozing. I don't like using people."

In fact, I get the same basic objections when I tell people they need to network.

Objection 1: Someone I know got a job by sending in a resume, so don't tell me I need to network to be successful.

Okay, so I get that people occasionally get hired from resumes. But the thing is, you don't just want one job — I hope. You want to build a career with lots of options for yourself, and building a strong network is the best way to do that. Even if you get one job from sending a resume, your network will help you get an EVEN BETTER job next time. What's more, it will give you the power and flexibility to choose work that interests you. Plus, networking is not just about getting jobs. You will gain valuable knowledge and insights into the world you live in, and this knowledge will help you map where you want your career to go.

Objection 2: Networking only works for white dudes.

There are gendered dimensions to networking, and they suck. When I started building my network with the app Shapr, most of the people who met me for coffee were men. Meeting men was easy, especially for me. It's a form of privilege that men, especially white men, have. And yes, that does make it easier. This is what sucks about networking. Because it's not this easy for everyone. Women, especially, have to face a lot of crap. Unwanted advances on social platforms — even "professional" platforms like LinkedIn. Attempts to reach out to males in positions of power, only to have it turned back into creepy flirting. I am so sorry this happens. It's not fair, and who am I to tell you to push through it and do it anyways? Men who are reading this might be surprised. Those who identify as women will not be shocked in the least.

But I do want to encourage you to find a way to make it work for you, no matter who you are. The unfortunate reality is that networking really is an absolute necessity for building a career in the twenty-first century, especially for those of us with less experience. I talked above about redefining networking, focusing on trying to have meaningful and intentional conversations. Try to find a way to make those happen within your comfort zone.

If you are having a networking meeting, an "informational interview," don't be afraid to insist on a situation that makes you comfortable. If you're not comfortable with an evening glass of wine, insist on a morning coffee instead. For the record, nobody has ever asked me to network over an evening glass of wine. You can always suggest a call if you prefer. Try reaching out to women who are more established in their career and attending women's networking events. If you are a member of a visible minority, you might choose to focus your efforts on reaching out to minority executives, at least to start. I know several executives of different identities who choose to focus their mentoring on a specific group: women, BIPOQ LGBTQ+, etc.

Find a way to be comfortable networking and try your best to let the crap roll off your back. It will be transformative for your career and create more options than you can imagine. Don't give up. It will be so worth it, I promise. And don't give up on the white guys either. There are a lot of us white men who are trying our best to use our privilege to subvert the dominant power structures and make more room at the table for everyone. You'll likely know pretty quick when you talk to someone if they're honestly caring and want to help you or if they have an ulterior motive. Trust your gut.

Objection 3: Networking is transactional.

It can be and, based on my description of it above, it might seem so. But I don't think of networking as strictly transactional. It may be idealistic, but I like to think of networking as trying to understand another human being. It's as much anthropology as economics. You're learning about their world and their identity, trying to understand if it connects to you at all and, if so, how.

Usually, networking feels like making a work friend. If you've ever worked a job, you understand this. Or you might have a similar experience with a fellow student or lab mate. These are people you wouldn't normally be "friends" with, but you build a sort of relationship so that you can work together amicably. You'll happily chat at the water cooler and ask them how their weekend was, but you don't get together for BBQs. There's nothing wrong with this. Both of you understand what is expected and, aside from an occasional office outing, you probably never see them outside of work. That's okay. It doesn't mean you're just using them or that you're a bad person for keeping them at arm's length. You can still enjoy their company. It's just a natural part of work relationships.

Objection 4: I don't have anything to offer.

Some people don't want to network because they imagine that it's transactional, but also because as a part of this transaction, they don't feel like they have anything to offer. I know I just said networking isn't transactional, and I don't think it has to be. But if it were, you don't need to feel like you have nothing to offer. As I said above, you never know where a career will take you. Right now, you're an unemployed PhD. Next week you might be a director of research or vice president of a company. Don't sell yourself short.

If nothing else, you can offer a great conversation. You can make that person feel validated in the work they do by showing how interested you are. You can ask them lots of questions, and that may cause them to reflect on their career trajectory and decisions they've made.

At its best, networking should be like the conversation you strike up with an interesting person beside you on the plane. It should be like someone on campus that you don't know well but love chatting with when you bump into them. It can be invigorating, exciting, and inspiring, and hopefully won't be too intimidating.

So, don't get business cards printed. Don't even go to networking events if you don't want to (or at least avoid events that are called "networking events"). Just focus on meeting people in any way you can. Follow them on Twitter and send them a note. Add them to LinkedIn. Email them at their company email address if it's posted online. Go to conferences and meetings where you'll meet people. Ask your family members if they could introduce you to someone, or maybe ask your supervisor or another professor.

And in time, you may even — *gasp* — learn to like networking!

* * *

Above, I quoted the old adage, "Your network is your net worth." But what does that even mean? It's an old cliché that we don't really get — until you see it in action.

One day in fall 2019, I had a coffee with a well-connected Ottawa man. Sitting in a Tim Horton's coffee shop in a Hawaiian shirt and cargo shorts, he told me exactly what was possible with my PhD. Up until this point, I was flailing. Only days earlier I'd had the meeting with Jim the realtor, and I was certain that I couldn't even cut it even as a realtor. I felt like I wasn't slick enough to sell houses.

The coffee with — let's call him Charles — opened up a whole world of possibilities.

"What do you want to do?" Charles asked.

"I'm not sure," I replied. "To be honest, I was hoping you could give me some ideas of what I can do with a PhD in Ottawa."

He laughed. "Anything you want. What are you interested in?"

I shrugged. "I don't know."

"Do you like politics? You could work as a policy advisor for a cabinet minister."

I nodded, hardly believing such a thing was possible. "Yeah, that sounds interesting."

"Or how about think tanks or public affairs?" He pulled out his Blackberry and started flipping through his LinkedIn app. Within five minutes, he had listed ten people I needed to talk to.

One of the people he told me about was an executive at a think tank (also with a PhD). When I got home, I looked her up and sent her a LinkedIn message:

Hi NAME,

My name is Chris Cornthwaite. I'm just about to defend my PhD and new to Ottawa. I'm exploring where I want my career to go next. Although I'm a great researcher, I'm best with connecting to people. Charles recommended you to me, and I'm so glad he did. It seems that we have a similar skill set, and I would absolutely love to have a coffee with you to ask you some questions. Would you be interested in meeting, even for twenty minutes? I know this is a big ask, and I thank you for considering it either way.

Sincerely, Chris

I don't think it's particularly good, and I wouldn't write the same thing today. It wasn't perfect, but it didn't have to be. The response came back anyway. She asked for a resume. They needed someone to start that week. There were a number of projects they were behind on.

When she emailed back, she said: *It's short notice, but is there any way you could come in for an interview at 9:00 tomorrow morning? If not, we can do next week.*

I emailed back: *I'll be there at 9:00.*

I was there, and I got the job. They desperately needed someone. I proved myself quickly and was offered a full-time, permanent job several months later, with a pension and benefits.

I built my network, timidly at first, and then more boldly. When I started work for the think tank, I had a strange experience. Those people who I had been hesitant to talk to weeks earlier now wanted to talk to me.

I met with one man who worked for a lobbying group. He had kindly agreed to meet with me before I ever had a job but asked if we could meet in a month. By the time we had our meeting, I had been hired at the think tank.

As we sat over coffee, I explained the projects I was working on. One in particular was a round table with some business leaders and politicians he wanted to work with. After I finished explaining to him what the event would look like, he spoke.

"I know there will be a lot of people there, and you may have the guest list set. But if it's possible, I'd really love to come."

A month earlier, I had been reaching out to him, desperately hoping he would have a coffee with me. Now, he was asking me if I could include him in a project I was running. And do you know what the worst thing was? I had to say no! He reached out to me by email a week later asking again if he could come, and once again I had to say no. It was awkward and uncomfortable, and I hated it. But it wasn't my choice. The government was paying for the project and they didn't want any lobbyists there.

It was an important lesson in how quickly a power dynamic can change. This is why I said above that you never know where the world and your career will take you. Intelligent people of all stripes understand this. You may be in a position of power six months from now, and the person you just met might be out of a job and need you to connect them.

Talk to everyone. Don't be too good for anyone. If someone acts too good for you, move on. It's not an indictment of you personally, but perhaps an indication that they're either not interested, too busy, dealing with family drama, or just have issues. There are always people who are hungry to connect to power and ignore others, just like there are always people at academic conferences walking around looking at your nametag to decide if you're worth talking to (I usually wasn't worth talking to).

Don't take it personally. Keep trying.

Your network evolves in time. You'll enter it as a tiny little grad student, scared of what the world will bring and feeling like a loser as you click "send" on message after message, many of which don't come back to you. Then, it will start to grow and build on itself. You will develop not only familiarity to the people in your network, but also a reputation (hopefully a good one).

From my first few cold emails and LinkedIn messages asking strangers for coffee, my network grew to include some powerful and successful people who I really look up to.

* * *

I can't resist citing a bit of my research, which was in immigrant trade networks. I found again and again that social capital was tremendously important for holding social groups together and for dictating who someone trades with. People do business with people they trust. Pierre Pierre Bourdieu's famous description of social capital is as follows:

> *Social capital is the aggregate of the actual or potential resources which are linked to possession of a durable network of more or less institutionalized relationships of mutual acquaintance and recognition – or in other words, to membership in a group – which provides each of its members with the backing of the collectivity-owned capital, a 'credential' which entitles them to credit, in the various senses of the word. These relationships may exist only in the practical state, in material and/or symbolic exchanges which help to maintain them. They may also be socially instituted and guaranteed by the application of a common name (the name of a family, a class, or a tribe or of a school, a party, etc.) and by a whole set of instituting acts designed simultaneously to form and inform those who undergo them; in this case, they are more or less really enacted and so maintained and reinforced, in exchanges. Being based on indissolubly material and symbolic exchanges, the establishment and maintenance of which presuppose re-acknowledgment of proximity, they are also partially irreducible to objective relations of proximity in physical (geographical) space or even in economic and social space.*[16]

Building social capital is a combination of building trust and becoming perceived as belonging to a social group, which is constructed through rituals, modes of being, rites of passage, and so on. Bourdieu's work also explains why there's so much economic return for becoming a known commodity in a network: having social capital increases your ability to leverage economic capital.[17]

If you skipped that academic-speak in the last paragraph, let me just say this. Building a network is basically building your social capital. Furthermore, it's building a network of trust; people trust you and you trust them. For this reason, I guard my network. I take it very seriously, and I take my position in it seriously. I trust the people in my network, and I hope they trust me.

Now, I don't mean that I trust them to watch my kids while I go on vacation. I trust their competence and connectivity in their industry. When they share thought leadership on LinkedIn or when I see them on the news or hear them on the radio, I trust what they have to say. I value it. I hope they feel the same way about me.

I try not to do anything that violates that trust. On Twitter, I'm flippant, provocative, and emotional. But on LinkedIn — where I mostly engage with my network — I'm guarded and careful.

Is this being fake or two-sided?

I don't think so. Honestly, it's being intelligent about knowing my audience and how I present myself.

If they wanted to, they could easily look at my Twitter and realize the double life that I'm leading. I'm not especially worried about this; in fact, it would likely add credibility that I can exist in both worlds.

* * *

So how do you build a network?

Start with your accidental network

You already have a network. It looks different depending on who you are, but you do know family, friends, former colleagues, alumni of your program, and professors you studied with. Each of these people has things they know about the world of work, and some of them might be worth a conversation.

Talk to them and see what they do. Use the "informational interview" format and ask them questions like:

1. What is your job like?
2. How did you get into your position?
3. What are the hardest or most discouraging parts of your work?
4. What are the most encouraging parts of your work? What do you love?
5. How would someone get into a position like yours?
6. Where do you think your career might go next?

7. What advice would you have for someone in my position?

8. Can you give me a sense of what some salaries might look like for someone like me in your industry?

9. Who else should I talk to?

10. Does your company hire consultants? If so, how?

Each of these gives you insight into their world of work and helps you learn about possibilities.

Also, ask these people you know for introductions to others. Your professors, in particular, may be a great source of network contacts to people working outside of academia. Many professors dabble in industry, sit at policy roundtables, and advise government. You might be surprised at who they know. If one is hostile to non-academic careers (which some are), try another one until you find someone who will connect you. An introduction goes a long way.

LinkedIn

After you've exhausted your list of existing contacts and asked for connections to interesting people, you can leverage LinkedIn as a powerful network-building tool. I recommend making your profile look good first; a professional and interesting profile will increase the chances that someone will connect with you. (There are free guides for how to do that on Roostervane.)

Once you've done this, send requests to people asking them to connect. It could read something like this:

> Hi NAME,
>
> I'm a recent graduate of X program. I'm trying to figure out how to turn it into a career, and the work you're doing looks really interesting. The EXAMPLE INITIATIVE, in particular, seems like a ground-breaking way to approach X PROBLEM. I know you're busy, but I would really love to chat for twenty minutes to ask a few questions about the industry. Would that be okay?

Thanks
Your NAME

The beautiful thing about these sorts of reach-outs is that it allows you to build your network intentionally. You can pick people doing work that you find interesting and try to connect with them.

And how do you find these people? Here are a few of my best tips:

- Type one of your skills into the LinkedIn search bar at the top and click "people." See what type of work people are doing with that skill.
- Go to the company page of organizations you would like to work at and click "people." It will show you employees who work there (including whether you have any contacts who are connected there), and you can connect with them.
- Join groups that are relevant to your desired career path and look at the group members. You can reach out to interesting people, leading with, "Hey, I saw you in the X group!"

LinkedIn can be intimidating for PhDs, but there is nothing else like it for building your brand and your network. Connecting to the people and opportunities there will change your life.

Other Social Media

There's nothing like LinkedIn for building a network, however, you can still benefit from other social media platforms. I'll mention two in particular: Twitter and Instagram.

Twitter

It's both wonderful and terrible. It's where all the most vile and disgusting side of humanity hangs out, and I know influencers who have been driven off of the platform by the abuses they faced. Having said that, if you can handle it, there are opportunities to connect there. I'd fill out a profile with your real name and photo (if you're comfortable) and follow interesting people, especially people active in your city or desired field. Don't be afraid to engage with them and reach out via a message if the opportunity arises.

Instagram

Instagram is a generally positive platform, but it's most effective for creatives. So if you're trying to break into a creative field — writing, photography, graphic design, art, speaking, etc. — it might be the platform for you. You can follow interesting people and send them a message. For example, one friend of mine wanted to become a children's book illustrator, and she messaged all of the best illustrators she could find on Instagram. Most of them wrote back with encouragement and tips on getting her work seen, and they're now friends.

Networking Apps and Sites

Shapr, the networking app, was a gift to me. If you've never seen it, it's like a Tindr for networking. You swipe right or left based on whether you want to meet the person. I put the best picture I could possibly find in some details about my title (PhD Candidate), a short description saying that I was new to Ottawa and trying to meet people, and a note on my interests that included traveling and photography, then I waited.

I swiped through the first fifteen profiles, impressed by what I saw. People with big, impressive job titles like policy analyst, chief economist, and even professor. I swiped like crazy and asked anyone who I matched with if they'd go for a coffee with me.

The results were impressive. A string of coffees with people with great jobs, each of whom were willing to tell me about Ottawa and all the great opportunities here. As I shared above, one suggested that I might enjoy working for a think tank and offered to make a personal introduction. Another asked if I'd be interested in politics; they knew a lot of people on Parliament

Hill and made the introduction to several high-powered people in Ottawa who would eventually shape my career. Others talked about governments and non-profits. One asked on the spot if I could do a job that they had open (I couldn't — there was way too much data involved) and weeks later gave me a referral on another job that got me an interview. One was from Shopify and offered to help any time I wanted to work there.

These were all coffees with strangers, which led to surprising results. Because most people are kind and generous and really do want to help people. It makes them feel good. I love to help people when I can. If I can make an introduction or refer someone for a job, I will. This is why networking works so well.

* * *

One of the hardest things I discovered about networking, as I mentioned above, is that you're not usually building a friendship with someone. You go out for coffee, have an hour conversation about life, work, and so on. And then you add each other to LinkedIn and you only speak again if you need something. It's weird and antithetical to all my being. I love building relationships with people, and it's hard when you enjoy a conversation and know that it's not something you'll likely do on a regular basis.

If there's any part of networking that's gross, this is probably it. People think that networking is handing out business cards at some sort of mixer. I've been to a few of these since coming to Ottawa and believe me, nobody likes to be there. And nobody likes the guy (yes, it's always a guy) who walks into a circle of people and hands every person his business card. Don't be that guy. Networking really is about connecting to another human being, and I love that part. You try to understand them and what makes them tick. But you don't call the person for lunch once a week.

Once you've made a connection, it's powerful. Because that connection you made just sits there. You occasionally like something they post on LinkedIn. You might see them on the street and smile and say hello. It might go on like this for a year or more. Then, there will come a day when you have a question for them, or you need something. Perhaps you'll see a job that looks perfect on LinkedIn and see that they are connected to the one hiring. Or perhaps you're an entrepreneur and you'll see a Request for Proposals through someone they're connected to. Maybe you'll just have a question about their industry.

Your connection, like a sleeper agent, can be activated. You'll drop them a note, perhaps with a cursory "hope you are well." Then you'll ask, "What do you know about the job at X company?"

And they'll say, "Oh yeah. I know the hiring person. Let me put you in touch with them."

It works just like this for anything related to your professional life. In January of 2020, I needed a lawyer for an incorporation, as well as a trademark lawyer. I searched "lawyer" in my LinkedIn search box. Within five minutes, I had messaged two of my lawyer connections and had suggestions for two top-notch Ottawa lawyers in each of these areas.

Two more networking tricks . . .

1. Ask for referrals

Don't be afraid to ask for referrals... all the time. One of my favorite things to do is to ask for a referral to another contact. Usually when I'm talking to someone — let's call her Claire — and explaining who I am and what I'm doing, she will say something like, "Oh that's really interesting, you should talk to Elizabeth who runs the R&D department at General Applify (my made up company)."

I'll make a mental note of it and as we're finishing our conversation say, "Oh, you said I should talk to Elizabeth! Would you mind introducing me to her?"

The answer is usually "Yes." The process usually works like this.

Claire goes and emails Elizabeth to say that they met someone who is interesting and wants to have coffee, then asks if it's okay to connect. Elizabeth ideally writes back that she will. Claire then emails both of us something like:

Hi Chris and Elizabeth,

I've spoken to both of you separately and I think you should meet. I think you'd have a lot to talk about.

Chris — Elizabeth runs the R&D department at General Applify. She's got a PhD as well, and there's nobody as well positioned as her to tell you about the research environment in Toronto.

Elizabeth — Chris is a new PhD graduate from U of T. He's interested in learning more about R&D since his PhD was in sociology, and he'd be keen to learn from you.

I'll leave the ball in your court. Hope it works for you to meet!

Cheers,

Claire

That's it. That's how warm connections are made! From this, I usually email both back separately, thanking Claire for her time and the referral, and indicating to Elizabeth how excited I am to meet her and asking to set up a time.

2. Use your network to get interviews

The other really cool thing you can do is use your network to get interviews! I referred to this above, but here's how it works. If I were to see that IBsoft is hiring, I would go on LinkedIn and see if I know anyone who is connected to anyone at that company. I don't reach out to the hiring manager directly. But I do message my network contact that I made:

Hey Jasmine,

Hope you are well. I saw the announcement for the Prosperous Cities project on LinkedIn and it looks fantastic! I'm sure it will be a huge success!

I was looking at the position that IBosoft has open right now. I'd be curious to chat with someone over there to get some more information, and I saw that you know Maurice. Would you be comfortable introducing me to him?

Thanks,

Chris

This is it, and usually the person will say yes unless they have a good reason not to. If they say no, don't sweat it. Just thank them and move on. While you'd be tempted to think that this means they don't think you're a good fit for the role, you never know what's going on. They may know something you don't about the position or the company – it might not be about you at all. They might be trying to protect you without saying out loud "that company exploits all its workers" or "it's going to fold in three months." Just do your thing and keep moving.

People want to talk to you

Students who are trying to network their way into a career are often tempted to write emails as if they were supplicants approaching a deity. You've seen a similar thing in academia, and likely employed such an approach in letters to prospective supervisors. Do not include sentences like, "I'm so sorry for wasting your time" or "I totally understand if you're too busy to respond to this." But do feel free to thank them for any time they can give you and be polite.

There's an interesting psychology at play here. If you position and carry yourself as an equal, you will get a better response than if you position yourself as someone who is socially inferior. Be confident in your tone and act as if you are a potential colleague instead of a beggar — because it's true.

Most people in the world of work are hungry to connect to other people. Some see it as a chance to pay forward the blessings they've had. Some might recognize your potential and know you'll be a connection worth having. Some might be scoping for a new position at their company and thinking that meeting with a PhD in their field will help them think it through. Some just love to chat. You will find people who want to connect to you. You'll be surprised at who does.

To this day, even though I'm a PhD with a great educational track record and spent time working for both a powerful Ottawa think tank and the government, I get nervous. My mouse hovers over the LinkedIn "connect" button and I tell myself the usual objections:

What if I'm not good enough?

What if they ignore me?

What if this hurts my brand because they think I'm a joke?

I can come up with a long list of my own shortcomings. It's pretty easy, really. Imposter syndrome never completely leaves us. Yet I'm constantly surprised by how willing people are to connect. Even more surprising, I've been around long enough that I've now connected to people who ignored my first request over a year ago. Some don't remember. Some will say, "Oh yeah, I saw your request and meant to respond, but it got buried in my inbox!" No matter what the story is, it never matches the story of my own inadequacy I was telling myself in my head.

So be like Jim, who I started the chapter with. Connect as if your career depends upon it. Because it does.

9

BUILDING YOUR BRAND

One of my favorite academics is Brené Brown, who has built an empire talking about shame and courage. She has a PhD in social work and is in high demand as a speaker, commanding huge sums of money. She rose to fame through a TED talk called "The Power of Vulnerability," and has appeared on Oprah's *Super Soul Sunday.* She had a cameo in the 2019 movie, *Wine Country,* and has her own Netflix special. She's a sought-after thought leader in the business community, and if you're not following her on LinkedIn, you should be!

In my own field of religious studies, a scholar named Reza Aslan had been active in the public domain, but he rose to fame when he was interviewed on the Fox News show *Spirited Debate* by host Lauren Green, about his book, *Zealot: The Life and Times of Jesus of Nazareth.* Green grilled Aslan about why he, a Muslim, would be interested in writing about Jesus. Aslan's calm and measured expert responses, as Green became more and more flustered and visibly angry, made the video go viral, and prompted follow-up interviews for Aslan with media outlets around the world. The exposure made Aslan a religious studies superstar, if such a thing exists, and he eventually hosted the show *Believer* on CNN.

Both examples of academics who have shot to popular appeal reveal something to us about the nature of value and how expertise is perceived. Is Brené Brown the world's best social work scholar? I don't know, but I doubt it. (Obviously, this would be an impossible metric anyway.) She would probably say the same. Does she command enormously high speaking fees because she's the most published in prestigious journals? Probably not. In the same vein, is Reza Aslan the world's best religious studies scholar? Nope. I'm a religious studies scholar, and I feel qualified to say that he wouldn't even break the top ten.

But both Brown and Aslan have something that most scholars do not, which makes them a valuable asset both to their institutions and to the public. They have a brand. Despite the fact that both of them apparently shot to fame primarily from one exposure — a TED Talk and a news interview — I promise you that they're not accidental celebrities. Both worked for years to build their personal brand, and those individual moments in time seen around the globe are the culmination of that work.

As you probably know, many academics turn their noses up at public scholars, as if they've sold out. They'll talk about how their work is sub-par and how their last peer-reviewed publication was heavily criticized. And it could be true! But guess what? It doesn't matter! And that professor bad-mouthing the celebrity academic is probably tremendously jealous of them since they gave their last conference presentation in front of thirteen people.

The lesson I'm trying to get at here is not that you need to be a celebrity scholar. On the contrary, I suspect most of us won't be. But in a world where PhDs are undervalued and underemployed, these scholars command high-paid speaking gigs, TV shows, and movie cameos. They're the type of scholars that non-academics who meet you will know. We'd do well to pay attention to what we can learn from scholars who are in super-high demand both inside and outside of the academy. They've built a brand — heck, they ARE a brand! And most PhDs are worried they'll be working at Starbucks when they're done.

I believe that you need to be a brand. I'm not saying you need to be a public intellectual who's on CNN every night, but one of the greatest ways to ensure your survival and thriving outside of academia is to become a brand. (It doesn't hurt your chances inside, either.)

This can look like a million different things. This might mean that you're the expert on Southeast Asian foreign policy in tight circle of Washington policy wonks. It might mean that you're the go-to person on childhood obesity in Wilmington, North Carolina. You might be the leading expert in a niche AI subject in Austin, Texas or Waterloo, Canada, or maybe you're the person to talk to about cyber security in Indonesia. Maybe you'll be the English PhD who becomes the person in Des Moines, Iowa that everyone reaches out to for solid copywriting.

Your niche and desired impact are for you to decide. Whether you want to stick with your PhD research and build off it or whether you want to branch out and become a thought leader in a new area is up to you. As I write this, the globe is engulfed in a pandemic, bringing the role of epidemiologists into the spotlight. For the first time, we can name doctors who specialize in infection control since they appear on the nightly news. They are new brands entering the public sphere.

Why you need to be a brand

So, what does a personal brand do for you anyway? I'm so glad you asked. I want you to imagine for a minute that instead of looking for jobs and having to apply, people would come to you and offer you jobs. I want you to picture a world where you could get consulting offers coming to you at such a high number that you'd have to turn people away or raise your rates. Imagine being asked to speak at a conference or give a presentation, and they plan it around your schedule. Imagine book publishers coming to you and offering you a publishing deal without you having to query them. Imagine starting a business and having money lined up and committed before you begin. Imagine never having to send out a resume again.

This is what branding does. Whatever thing you want from this life, whatever job you want to get or impact you want to have, branding will help you get it faster and more effectively than if you just chase it. When you become the person associated with knowledge and expertise in whatever field you choose, people will come to you. According to Douglas Kruger, a speaker and writer I enjoy, people achieve expert — or even guru — status when they have three things: Knowledge, Personality, and Publicity.[18]

Most academics have *knowledge*, but some need to adapt their knowledge to an area that's in some sort of demand in the real world. This doesn't mean that you need to study marketing, but it does mean you'll need to find the people who want to know what you know. The internet has made this easier than ever since you can find people who are interested in just about every niche. Dame Mary Beard is a world-famous classicist who appears frequently in the media and speaks around the world. She's also very active on Twitter. She's a tenured professor at Cambridge, so she'd have an income whether she was famous or not.

However, Mary Beard doesn't have more than two hundred and fifty thousand Twitter followers because she's a classics professor at Cambridge. She's engaging. She brings her knowledge and expertise to the public domain and presents it in a way that people love to hear. She has *personality* and, as a result, she's famous — deservedly so. You don't need to be famous, but you do want to be known as someone who's distinct and interesting. Ideally, according to Kruger, you aim to become the person in your field that people will tell their friends, "You need to talk to them." Whatever your field is, whatever the thing you do, when you get to this point money, work, and jobs will come to you... you won't have to chase.

The final piece of Kruger's triad is *publicity*. And while so many academics hate famous academics, and most human beings feel gross about chasing publicity, it's a vital one. Mary Beard does this on Twitter, of course, but she also appears in TV shows and in popular culture in a way that brings her knowledge to people who wouldn't otherwise hear it. So, let me be clear, *publicity* here does not mean greasy PR or bad radio ads. But you do need to get in front of people, often. This is easier than ever in the age of the internet. Twenty years ago, if you were passionate about the mating rituals of grasshoppers, you'd be hard-pressed to find anyone who would listen to you talk about it unless you were lucky enough to get on public radio or television. With the advent of the internet and social media, you have instant access to a world of people who are interested in the obscure things that you know. Go find them and build a crew

When we take *knowledge, personality,* and *publicity,* it makes a good roadmap for our path from degree to career as well. We have knowledge of some field, and perhaps we can take this and apply it to our non-academic career. This is often the case with people who have STEM specialties, but it's not limited to them. I know people who studied Shakespeare who work in theaters. I was a student of ancient diasporas who worked for the Department of Immigration. In these cases, some or all of your knowledge transfers to the non-academic space. Some PhDs take their knowledge of writing and editing, running projects, or leadership into the non-academic world. These PhDs still work in a knowledge domain too; they just don't necessarily use their PhD subject matter.

Personality is the thing that takes a body of knowledge and makes it personal to the way you present it. This DOES NOT mean you have to be bubbly and outgoing if you're not. Rather, personality is the thing that makes your use of the knowledge domain unique, no matter how that works. I know certain people who are renowned in public policy circles who speak like boring academics. Every time I see them interviewed on the news, I want to go to sleep. Or they post very formally-written things on LinkedIn. This personality conveys expertise and authority to people, even if it isn't bubbly and friendly. Be yourself, whatever that looks like, and find and nurture your voice.

Finally, publicity. We are living in a time where generating publicity has never been easier. When I started tweeting about non-academic careers for graduate students in October 2019, I had fifty followers. (I had been a lurker on Twitter for years.) By January 2020, I had five thousand. Now, of course, I also had an in-demand niche; there are lots of graduate students concerned about their future. But the use of social media has made it easier than ever for academics to develop followings of people who love what they do.

If you want publicity, define what your knowledge is and think about your personality a bit. Then get online and start creating content and thought leadership. Post on LinkedIn and connect with leaders in your chosen field, as well as potential customers. Create a Twitter, Instagram, or Facebook brand that's consistent with what you do. Find your crew and give them your knowledge. If you have a PhD in bird migration patterns, start tweeting (pun intended) about it and find bird-watcher groups to engage with. If you study medieval clothing, find people who love to see medieval clothing! Start an Instagram account with pictures of people dressed in medieval clothing! (I would straight up follow this right now, and I'm not the least bit interested in medieval clothing as a discipline.)

Also, don't forget about traditional media. You can pitch op-eds easily, no matter what your field of interest. A lot of people think the media is some guardian of power and authority that they could never have access to. The truth is that journalists are always looking for a story. Don't be afraid to give them one. (As an experiment, if your LinkedIn looks professional, go send connections to five media people and watch what happens!) The media is looking for thought leaders and experts all the time. Be that person.

How to build your brand

When you build a brand, it's true that opportunities come to you. Not everyone knows where to start to build it. Fortunately, I'm married to a brand builder who helps me to think about this all the time and calls me back when I go off brand. Here are a few specific tips on building your brand:

1. Decide your realm of expertise and stick to it

I decided last year that my posting online would be primarily about building careers and finding your purpose. Once this was established, I've focused on this niche. When I engage on social media, I try to keep this clear. Although I'm interested in other topics like politics, I don't share this on my Twitter, the platform I use most. I've chosen to have personal brand that is about careers.

Too many people try to be all things to all people. When you follow someone for an interesting post about politics, only to find them ranting about a terrible restaurant in Milwaukee the next day, you'll probably unfollow quickly.

People are concerned that if they focus on something, they'll lose followers or get pigeonholed. The opposite is true. When you focus, you define your expertise and tell your followers what to expect. When you're consistent, they'll keep coming back. It doesn't mean you can't evolve over time, but it should mean you aren't all over the place. If you're an expert in online education, stick with that. This is the essence of building a brand. Coca-Cola doesn't try to sell you cars along with soft drinks. Brand confusion is a sure way to lose influence and market positioning.

2. Find your platform

As I just mentioned, I spend most of my time on Twitter. I'm increasingly on Instagram and LinkedIn, but Twitter is my first love. For all the crap, I genuinely enjoy the platform. It's well-positioned to share ideas and thoughts, especially articles, and for me, it's a great place to engage. My spouse, Carolyne, hates Twitter and spends most of her time on Instagram. She's a graphic designer, so Instagram is a great place to share highly visual content and be creative. Twitter is terrible for images — I've found through experience.

I haven't mentioned Facebook yet. I personally don't like Facebook as a creator. It makes you pay to advertise to your own followers, and generally it's more of a casual social platform than a serious networking and employment one. If your grandma or your racist uncle are going to comment on your posts, it's likely not the place to engage with potential clients or employers. However, Facebook is still the biggest platform out there, and I've realized that the future of Roostervane will require driving traffic from there. If you are creating content that's directed to the general public — say you want laypeople to understand astronomy or do chemistry experiments for kids — Facebook is probably your platform.

It doesn't necessarily matter which platform you choose, but I would probably pick one or two at the most. Trying to be everywhere is great if you're expanding and growing a business with a whole marketing team, but as an individual thought leader it gets to be too much.

3. Find your crew

Find your group of people who care deeply about the same stuff, who hang out in the same spaces online, who are working towards some similar goal, and who speak each others' language. A related word is *niche,* which refers to the small corner of any marketplace that you might seek to build your identity and expertise in. Your goal is to find people who are like you, broadly speaking. These are the people who are interested in what you have to say and will be the base for building your brand.

You may exist in different crews. I'm an academic and that world makes sense to me. But I also love business, and I really enjoy talking to en-trepreneurs and business-minded people, whether they run websites or organic vegetable stands. I've also worked in public policy in Ottawa, a very unique and insular space, and I can kick it with the best of them there. There's nothing wrong with this. But in choosing which crew you want to serve, you'll likely choose only one. You can't be all things to all people. Choose the crew that you want to contribute to, to be a leader in, and devote your energy there.

4. Grow yourself

One dangerous thing about living in academia is that we associate learning with activities that happen in or around an institution. Whether you're in your degree or done, you should keep growing yourself. Never stop learning — strive to be the best in your industry at whatever it is you do. However, also grow yourself in areas that make you uncomfortable, but will make you better. This is something we academics don't do nearly enough. Why? Because the further we go, the more we get to choose what we learn. This can be great but can also mean that we learn narrow fields of knowledge. We don't always learn things that expand our possibilities. Learn public speaking, accounting, management, budgeting, which are basically skills that will make you better at whatever you do.

5. Identify your domain

Think through what geographical area your brand is a part of. Are you a local brand? Are you state/provincial? International? Since some of us are making use of the internet (frankly most of us should — it's a gift), we will have personal brands that stretch across geographies. This is great. But don't forget that with that comes more competition and, perhaps, less impact. You can be one of a thousand amazing experts in housing policy on Twitter, or you can be the top housing policy expert in your town (not mutually exclusive, by the way). Each of these may be worthy callings, but you might want to devote yourself to chasing one of them.

Be your authentic self

A few years ago, a video of Jane Goodall popped up on my Facebook feed. It's a video of a rehabilitated chimp being released back into the wild after near death. The chimp begins to move away, but then looks back at Goodall. It comes over, climbs up on the crate it was being transported in, and gives her a hug. The tender moment was shared around the world as Goodall returned the hug.

I knew who Jane Goodall was when I was a kid. In fact, she was the first scientist I could ever name. She wrote a series of children's books on various animal families, and I had *The Chimpanzee Family* on my bookshelf. On the back flap of the book was a picture of Goodall and a brief biography. That's why, for most of my young life, whenever I thought of a scientist, I pictured Jane Goodall in my mind.

Whenever I see Jane Goodall interviewed, there's one word that comes to mind: *authenticity*. I've rarely seen anyone care as much about anything as Jane Goodall cares about animals. It's her brand. She's passionate in a way that most humans aren't. After all, this is a woman who has made animals, especially primates, her life's work. Because of her authenticity, she's sought after in both academic and non-academic circles.

What is authenticity? Merriam-Webster defines authenticity in people as "true to one's own personality, spirit, or character." This is a good way to describe it, and this definition screams the reason why authenticity belongs in a chapter on branding. When people think of building a personal brand, they usually think of something canned and cold. They think of a marketing campaign or a buzzword and sometimes, to their detriment, try to recreate these. I've been guilty of this too.

Creating a personal brand can also be confusing for us because branding and marketing language is often used by people giving advice on non-academic careers. For example, we're commonly told to "practice our elevator pitch." Now, an elevator pitch can be a great thing when necessary, but it's just one more of the cold, stale, watered-down pieces of marketing advice that gets thrown at PhDs. The people giving this advice mean well, and there's nothing wrong with an elevator pitch. But if you adopt the idea that personal branding is an elevator pitch, I've got bad news for you.

It's these sorts of mistaken ideas about personal branding that create much of what I see on LinkedIn. I see people (not singling anyone out here) who post these god-awful humble brags about their accomplishments: "Delighted to be the keynote speaker at X;" "Had the privilege of being featured in Y;" or "Happy to participate in Z." Not surprisingly, these types of cold expressions don't get much traction. Again, I feel especially qualified to judge this because I've done it SO MANY TIMES!

Then there's Michaela Alexis. After losing her job in 2015, she turned to LinkedIn and created a career. Her article on how she created her dream job on LinkedIn went viral and she now has a hundred and fifty thousand followers. I love Michaela's content because she's fearless —she pours out her heart, her fears, and her wins on LinkedIn. And people respond. I've seen similar responses when people, at the end of their rope looking for a job, post vulnerably on LinkedIn about their struggles. Ironically, that can be the thing that finally gets them a job.

Academia can kill authenticity. It's one of the reasons why people like Brené Brown are such a breath of fresh air. When you find academics that are honest about their wins and their struggles and share their voice, you want to hear more. We're humans. We love this. Authenticity isn't image. It's letting the things you care about, that drive you, and that make up you deepest and truest self bubble over into your everyday life. I struggle with authenticity all the time. I'm scared to show the world the real me. In fact, I think a lot of humans are. That's why we find it so inspiring when people have the courage to be authentic. That's why we want to follow authentic leaders.

Build your brand. Don't be afraid to do it and take it seriously. I promise that it will make a tremendous difference in your search for reinvention. And don't be afraid to make your authenticity a part of it.

10

MONEY

I arrived in the lobby of the think tank and sat nervously. Tapping my fingers on a copy of their latest report I'd picked up from the coffee table, I sat in a plush chair waiting to be called. I felt out of place and nervous but tried my best to slow my breathing. I was all too aware that my suit was a bit wrinkled and didn't fit me right. I was too poor for a new one. I hoped they wouldn't notice.

My future boss led me down a hallway and into a nice conference room. We sat across from one another, and she asked me questions one by one. I did my best to confidently explain how I fit the role that I'd only heard about the day before. As the interview was ending, she asked if I had any questions for her. I asked a few about fit, the mission, organizational values, and finally the one I'd secretly been waiting to ask all along:

"What does it pay?"

She smiled. "I'd have to double check, but I think it should be between thirty-five and forty dollars an hour. Is that okay?"

I kept my composure and nodded, doing my best to suppress a smile. "Yes, that seems reasonable."

I didn't negotiate. I was doing the math in my head, realizing that I'd be making between $70,000 and $80,000 a year. From the point of deciding to leave the PhD right up until that moment, I figured I'd be lucky to make $40,000.

Now that seemed like an incredibly high number to me at the time. However, if I stop and consider what I made during my final PhD year, the comparison is interesting:

$35,000: *Big-ass scholarship*

$14,000: *Extra travel money*

$13,000: *Government grants (Thanks Canada)*

$5,000: *Other misc. funding*

That's $67,000 — and it wasn't taxable. From that $67,000, I had to pay about $8,000 tuition. All told, I had about $59,000 left to work with.

My first job paid something like $74,000, which sounds like a lot of money. And it is. It was twice what my dad made when I was a kid, and what he and my mom had to raise five kids with. But I realized pretty quickly that that income bracket pays a marginal tax rate of around 29 percent in Canada. After taxes, I was bringing home around $55,000, minus other deductions like pension and benefits. So, let's say I was bringing home $50,000 total. That's not a lot to live on for a family of five in Canada. Carolyne was bringing in a bit of income from her graphic design business, but it was just getting started.

We certainly didn't feel rich. And I still had a pile of student loan debts. I had big plans to pay them down as fast as I could, and I did start paying them. But there often wasn't much left at the end of the month, no matter how frugal we were. With three kids and a dog at home, we had enough surprise extra expenses like school trips and unexpected vet visits to keep us barely breaking even.

I was learning a valuable lesson. Creating financial security for yourself after a PhD isn't just about making a high salary. It's about playing financial catch-up for many lost years of earnings and savings and paying down debt. Financial catch-up isn't easy, no matter how large your income is after your PhD; you're going to have less to work with than you thought.

I started calculating my future. Sure, my income would go up quickly. But even if I made $90,000, I'd be bringing home around $66,000. If I made $110,000, I wouldn't bring home more than $78,000. I don't mind paying my fair share, but I realized that climbing out of my student debt hole and getting to the same financial level as my peers would take me at least a decade at the rate I was going. A decade of living in poverty, still feeling like a grad student, barely making ends meet. No matter how well you do after your PhD, the opportunity cost of doing a PhD can haunt you for a long time.

* * *

I often talk about money, and people are routinely upset with me for it. When they're making $35,000 a year, and I talk about making $70,000 in my first job, people who are already working outside of academia are understandably upset. Some think I'm bragging. Some see it as setting up unrealistic expectations. I get it. It hurts to have someone come along and say you should be making $70,000 when you're scraping by for $30,000.

I'm not trying to insult you or make you feel unworthy. But I insist on having these conversations. My understanding of my own worth influences yours, especially if you're a current PhD student. I once released a poll on Twitter that asked what people made in their first non-academic job out of their PhD. The results were surprising to some. Of the 941 people who responded to the poll, 565 made more than $60,000 in their first post-PhD job. HigherEdJobs estimates that the average assistant professor in the U.S. starts around $67,750.[19] Of the Twitter poll respondents, 60 percent were making starting assistant professor salaries, while at least 33 percent were making more. And 141 of the respondents, around 15 percent, started at over $100,000.

You NEED to know this, especially if you're a current student. You need to know what's possible. Because if all you hear is professors and fellow grad students telling you that you must pay your dues as an adjunct, you will believe you're worth $35,000. If you get congratulated for a $45,000 postdoc, you'll believe you're worth that. You'll celebrate over beer with friends for having achieved such a high academic milestone and wonder where to spend your new-found "wealth."

So, when the university rejects you for a tenure-track job and tells you you're not good enough, and you are tempted to think adjuncting is all you're worth, remember that many PhDs working in non-academic roles make the same as starting professors do and a third make more. This information is power. You might start to believe that you're worth more without even trying. If you do, then my job is complete. Because, as I said in chapter four, the entire academic system functions on you believing that you're worthless.

Knowing your worth is a revolutionary thing. It will change everything. If all grad students knew it, it would change the academy. They would fly out of there so fast that there would be nobody left to apply for the shitty adjunct courses. And the university might have to pay people a living wage to work there.

It comes down to our expectations. Our understanding of what's financially normal determines our reality. It's one reason why it can be so hard for those of us from poor backgrounds to break free. We spent our lives watching our parents scrape for nothing, fighting a world that was fundamentally tilted against them. I expected to live like my parents. I had a benchmark in my mind that told me that "normal" is scraping to get by. Academia fit that expectation really well. And now I'm working to change it.

Rules of Wealth for PhD Graduates

My dad was a maintenance man. My father in law, who was relatively successful by northern Ontario standards, was a planner at the paper mill. My mother-in-law was a nurse. All of the adults in my life had different incomes, but they all operated under the same basic wealth principles. They started in their twenties and put away a percentage of their paycheck for life. Each got a pension.

They are the exact type of people who often teach us about money — our parents. Many PhDs have family who are blue-collar. Our mothers, fathers, uncles, aunts, and cousins try to give us advice based on what worked for them. They tried to help us understand the world as they see it. And I'm afraid that PhDs, when they finish their degrees, are tempted to sink back into seeing the world the way their working-class parents did. But I don't think income and wealth will work the same for our generation as a whole, and definitely not for PhDs.

I don't want to talk much about the nuts and bolts of personal finance in this book. First of all, I'm not qualified. I'm not a financial planner. I've recommended various books on Roostervane, each of which I learned something from. I've learned that most personal finance books are the same, but different. Some want you to pay down debt in a debt snowball. Some want you to pay yourself first. Some want you to do extreme coupon clipping and savings until you can retire early. There are a million different ways to deal with your money. So what follows are not hard and fast rules, but they are observations I've made about PhD wealth. Feel free to disagree. And I ain't loaded yet, so take these with a grain of salt.

Rule 1: You must fight for a better money mindset.

I was raised to think "there's never enough money," and we'd scrape by on what we had, going without most things in the process. Furthermore, as religious people, my parents would moralize our poverty. We were "content with what we had," implying that desiring more would be sinful. We knew that "the love of money was the root of all evil," and "God provides what we need." Since nearly everyone in my town was poor, I learned from my blue-collar peers to hate the "rich motherfuckers" who owned the mines and the mills, and usually lived far away in Toronto. Then, when I finally broke free of my impoverished past and went to university, I learned from professors that the rich were exploitative and lived off the poverty of others. (Many of these profs were making over $150,000 a year, if you're keeping score.)

Is it any wonder I was terrified of wealth and associated it with all sorts of moral and societal evils? I was trained to hate it, to think implicitly, *I don't want it.* (Ironically, the many people who harped on the wealth in my hometown still seemed able to cough up $40 a week for lottery tickets.)

I was fortunate along my journey to meet some wealthy people. I realized something about them pretty quickly. They weren't greedy or evil. In fact, they were some of the most generous people I'd ever met. They made their money running businesses that employed people, putting food on the tables of dozens of families that wouldn't be there if they hadn't started their business. I knew one wealthy couple who on several occasions donated thousands of dollars to families in need in our community. The couple never told me this. The benefiting family accidentally let it slip one day.

Wealthy people, in fact, drastically repositioned my own understanding of wealth. I came to realize that wealth doesn't make you good or bad. It makes you a bigger version of who you already are. People who are assholes become wealthy assholes, people who are generous become incredibly generous. If you are filled with goodness and kindness, money amplifies your ability to be kind.

Your beliefs about money will dictate your relationship towards it. If you believe, even subconsciously, that having money makes you bad, or greedy, or is unspiritual, it's not much of a surprise that you will live in poverty. You'll sabotage your own financial success to get back to that place. If you believe that you're a good person and that money could both give you a great life and amplify your goodness, you will likely begin to acquire some.

For those of us who were raised poor, this mental shift is not easy. It's difficult to de-program all the money mindset you've learned over the years. But it can be done. Read money books. Get around wealthy people you admire, either in person or online. Try to identify where your beliefs about money came from. Ask yourself why you have them and if they're serving you well. And start to change them.

Rule 2: Spend less than you make.

At the end of the day, wealth — and the accumulation thereof — comes from a gap between spending and income. The bigger this gap, the more you can save. The more money you can put away, the more you can use to generate more money. If you make $100,000 and piss $99,000 of it away, you're financially behind someone who makes $50,000 and saves $5,000. (Obviously this comparison gets more complicated if they each buy assets.)

Rule 3: Divorce time from money.

There's something the working class doesn't understand about money. Heck, I think the middle class barely understands it. As long as time and money are tied together, your income will be limited. Growing up in a working-class town, we understood money in units of hours. If someone wanted to express to you just how rich someone was, they would give you their value in time. Jean makes seventy dollars an hour as a crane operator. Guy makes fifty-six dollars an hour operating an excavator. These people were the inconceivably rich ones.

Truly wealthy people learn to divorce their time from money. They build systems, machines, that earn them money when they're not working. Whether you like him or not, when you buy something on Amazon, Jeff Bezos gets money. Let that sink in. The person who owns the coffee shop down the street from you makes money when you buy coffee there, whether they're in the building or on the beach. Michael Jackson's songs are still making money, long after he died. Apparently, his estate made $74 million in 2015.

Inventors who license their patents make money when a company sells their product. When I lived in London, Ontario, there was an incredibly wealthy man who cruised around in old cars and lived on a beautiful estate. His father developed the technology that would lead to the birth control pill, and his son lives off the royalties decades later. In the same vein, authors who write books make money when someone buys that book, no matter what they are doing at the time. The internet has birthed a whole new generation of people who can separate time from money: YouTube stars, Instagram influencers, Twitter thought leaders, LinkedIn voices. As long as their platforms are monetized in some way, whether it's through selling products or marketing for affiliates, they are making money regardless of whether they're awake or sleeping.

One of the things I love about academia is that it actually teaches us to separate our time from money. I won a $100,000 grant once and the application didn't take much longer than the one that won me $15,000 the year before. I received that grant no matter how much research I did while I held it. This is a lesson that should carry with us into the real world.

University endowment funds bring in revenue every year without depleting the principle; that's why they're such a sustainable funding model (until the market crashes). You can build your own personal endowment fund too, believe it or not. People who save up huge chunks of money can live off the interest for the rest of their lives. This is separating time from money.

Rule 4: Serve as many people as possible (scale).

The more people you impact, the more money you will make. It's not a perfect science, but if you can scale the value you offer to people, you'll make a lot. I love personal finance, and I followed all the gurus: Dave Ramsey, Suze Orman, and David Bach were my favorites. I digested their wealth principles and tried to implement them in my own life. (I still think they have lots of interesting ideas). But I finally realized something. None of these financial gurus got rich from following their own advice, from putting aside portions of their paycheck every week or from paying down debt fast. They got rich because they impacted millions of people with their ideas, and their books and seminars have sold around the world. They massively leveraged their value and impact by reaching the masses.

It's not that these strategies don't work at all. But if you're thirty-five years old and have $100,000 in student debt, saving forty-five dollars a week in mutual funds isn't going to make you wealthy. You've got to play some catch-up. And what better way to catch up than to leverage your tremendous education, brainpower, and ideas into something that can influence lots of people. Build a platform. Create products. Get vocal and be noticed. Then find a way to make money off it. That's scale. Even PhDs who don't get academic jobs should be thinking about scale.

This book is a product. If I were to sell it for ten dollars, and two hundred people bought it, I'd have made $2,000 (assuming I keep all ten dollars). It's something but, since the book took me months to write, it probably wouldn't be a good value for my time. If a hundred thousand buy it, I'd have made a million dollars —a damned good investment on six months of work. Serve as many people as possible.

Rule 5: Build a brand.

Potato chips are a big deal in Canada. Every time I travel in the United States, I feel tremendous sympathy for the lack of delicious potato chip flavors there. One of my favorite flavors is all dressed. A Canadian brand called President's Choice (no, we don't have a president) makes the best all dressed chips on the market. Even though there are cheaper versions, I will pay double for these ones. Given the choice between Coke and Pepsi, I'll choose Coke every time. When I bought a car last year, I paid an extra $10,000 for a Honda, when I could have gotten a Chevy much cheaper.

Why would I do this? In food, I know what I like, and the brand signals to me that it's worth the extra price. When it comes to cars, the Honda brand name signals reliability and longevity, while Chevy makes me think of my first car — a Chevy Cobalt — that broke down frequently and fell apart. When it limped back onto the car lot for a trade in, I swore to myself I'd never buy another Chevy. The extra $10,000 was worth it to me for a Honda.

This is how brands work in a commercial setting, and there are many lessons for PhDs wanting to work outside of academia. I know PhDs who are leaders in their field, internationally respected outside of academia. For example, one whose specialty is AI gets invited to nearly every roundtable across the country. There are PhDs who are thought leaders who can consult at a rate of $1,000 a day. They command massive sums wherever they go and are in demand. Organizations clamor to make sure their name is on a report on their area of knowledge, *because if X did it, it's good*.

This, my friends, is a weird sort of PhD influencer you can be, and it comes from being a brand.

Rule 6: Learn to do something not a lot of people can do (scarcity).

Not sure if you took an Economics 101 class, but it's important to remember that things that are needed or desired, but not plentiful are valuable. You know this if you've ever tried to hire a plumber or buy a diamond ring. On the other hand, some things are plentiful but not really needed. Yes, I'm sorry to say my Humanities PhD fit into this category. Universities continually produce these degrees which have literally no demand in the marketplace (whether some of the skills are in demand is a different conversation). A PhD used to be rare, but when overproduction made the PhD itself a commodity held by many, it lost scarcity. Plus, the university hacked apart the way it delivers degrees while simultaneously producing more. Now PhDs have nowhere that they're really needed. No scarcity.

Five hundred people can do what you can do.

If this is depressing, good. Let it sink in for a minute. But then, realize this. Once you understand the principle of scarcity, or maybe a better way to say this is to recognize where the skills demands are, you can build a complementary skill set to your PhD that makes you super valuable.

My PhD in religious studies held minimal value in the marketplace — academic or non-academic. When I finished, I paid my dues running projects at a think tank. I'm now a PhD who knows how to both run and fund full-cycle research projects, scope issues, convene stakeholders, and write final reports to government (according to their guidelines). I can do all this with no supervision, in a town (Ottawa) where virtually every organization needs to put recommendations to the government. As my value grew, so did my job offers.

Academics have two basic ways to profit from scarcity in the non-academic marketplace.

First, they can know things nobody else does that have value in the marketplace, like T-cell cloning or polymer manipulation. This is usually the case for STEM graduates. Others like me, who have degrees with no direct demand, must leverage their skills into scarce marketplaces. We must be people who can do things that not a lot of people can. This might be running projects, editing at a high level, writing great copy, or being an engaging teacher.

Most academics never think this through.

The related idea here is that there are situations when a PhD gives you a competitive edge. There are lots of people who could hypothetically manage a complex research project. But someone with experience managing complex projects who also has a PhD might have an edge. In this case, your PhD might be an advantage. Because when people see the author of a report has a PhD, it means something. Lots of people can be policy advisors. But a policy advisor with experience and a PhD stands out. If you have a solid skillset plus a PhD, you can start to get some traction.

One other area I've found PhDs can have some scarcity is grant writing. It's something we do especially well and one of the areas most of us have some sort of a track record in. Few people with master's degrees can say that their grant writing has won tens or hundreds of thousands of dollars in grants.

Rule 7: Do complicated things (complexity).

If you're like most PhDs, your brain has been programmed to deal with complexity in a way that a lot of people can't. You will see the big picture of what a three-hundred-page manuscript is trying to accomplish, but you'll also notice the tiny grammatical error right in front of you. This is, in my estimation, one of the most valuable components of PhD training. Your brain can work at a level that most people are not trained to.

Handling complexity with minimal supervision is highly valued in the marketplace. It's what managers, presidents, CEOs, and other leaders do all day, every day. They look at organizations, understand how each part works, and drive it forward in such a way that it works together.

You probably have this skill set. You just need to stop trying to apply it to Chaucer and start learning to apply it to the marketplace. Learn some business basics. Take some finance courses. Take a project management course. Really, just find ways to show that you handle complexity in organizations – whether that's with complex projects, managing people, or dealing with budgets. The marketplace will reward you for it, and you'll end up doing things that are more and more complex.

Rule 8: Take control of your labor.

When you sell your time to an employer, they usually get the better value. Do you think they'd keep you around if they didn't? They can sell your labor for a premium that makes them money off the difference. If they couldn't do this, you'd be laid off quickly. You trade your actual labor value for the security of a paycheck and a pension. And the employer takes the risk, but also gets the reward.

If you're willing to forego a bit of security to start your own business and take control of your labor, you might do very well. (But don't let me fool you. It's a crap ton of work!) Consulting can be an incredibly lucrative career for PhDs. In this situation, you basically become self-employed and sell research, projects, advice, you name it to an employer for somewhere around the actual cost of what your labor is worth in the marketplace.

Rule 9: Wealthy people are further along, not different.

I can't stress this enough. Wealthy people are not a different species or existing in a different universe that you can never touch. They're simply further along in their journey. When you look at a senior professor, you don't say, "Oh wow, they have a hundred publications. I could never be like that." You say, "Someday I'll have that many publications too." You see the differences between the two of you as different waystations along the same journey.

What if you did this with wealthy people? What if, instead of hating on them or imagining that they got that way because they stepped on people, you saw them as simply further along the journey than you? This would be a much healthier way to approach it and would actually help you to realize that you can build wealth. Learn from wealthy people. Watch to see how they've used the rules above and see how those rules apply to your life.

These are my nine rules of wealth that I've learned and am working on implementing. As I write them, I'm struck by the wealth paradoxes in my society. We have a capitalistic system, but for some reason there is no course in school that will teach students how it works and how they can succeed in it. Many parents, like my own, are hamstrung by one traditional, almost puritanical idea: we don't talk about money. In all my years in school, the only money education I ever received was what I taught myself. You can choose whether you want to talk about it, but don't feel guilty about creating your wealth. Hunt down those mindsets that keep you from thinking about wealth in the first place. And when you get your wealth, use it to amplify your goodness.

11

ENTREPRENEURSHIP

L ast year I met Jim Balsillie, who co-founded Blackberry. I had heard people say negative things about Jim, but I found him to be an incredibly kind and down-to-earth man. He is also remarkably driven, fighting to protect Canadian startups from what he sees as predatory American multinationals. The truth is, I liked him a lot. When Blackberry was in its heyday, it turned the small city of Waterloo into a world tech hub. I used to visit Carolyne at the University of Waterloo when she was a student there. At the edge of the campus were some large buildings that were owned by Research In Motion (Blackberry). Most of Carolyne's friends would work at RIM during their degree. Undergraduates would do placements at Blackberry that paid thirty-five dollars an hour and would launch their careers in tech. Waterloo — a small city near Toronto — became the Canadian Silicon Valley.

Just as I was raised with a lot of assumptions about wealthy people, I was raised with a lot of ideas about entrepreneurs. I didn't know much about business. Actually, I don't think many people in my hometown did either. As I said above, we were the blue-collar people who worked for the mine or the mill, and our language was the paycheck and the pension.

In the tiny little part of Canada I grew up in, there aren't a lot of successful entrepreneurs. But there were a few. One guy in particular had sold his construction company for $10 million and built a beautiful house on a lake in a nearby town. Everybody knew exactly who he was and what he had done, and everyone had ideas about him. The word I heard thrown around the most was "lucky."

Yup, I was raised to believe that the few successful entrepreneurs out there were lucky. They were lucky because they were rich. They were rich because they were lucky. And I already told you the things we thought about rich people in the last chapter.

My blue-collar peers had different ideas about entrepreneurs who weren't rich yet, the ones still grinding away.

They were greedy, not willing to be content with a paycheck from the mine.

They were secretly unhappy.

They were overcompensating for something.

They were sacrificing their family lives to work.

They were stingy and didn't help the poor.

They liked to squeeze money out of people.

All these things formed an idea in my mind about my own solidarity with the working class. I belonged here, living in poverty but working nobly. I didn't want to be an entrepreneur, rich or poor. Why would I with all the terrible things I'd heard?

At a certain point in my life, I started meeting successful entrepreneurs. While they weren't in Jim Balsillie's league, they ran successful companies, mostly in landscaping and transportation. They were some of the kindest, most generous people I've ever had the chance of knowing. As I talked about in the last chapter, these entrepreneurs (also the rich people I know) were incredibly generous with their time, their money, and their possessions. To this day, I've never met anyone more giving of what they had.

In fact, the more entrepreneurs I've met, the more I wanted to be one. Successful entrepreneurs all have one thing in common: they add value to people's lives and are rewarded for it. (I get there there's some fuzzy applications of this around Wall Street. For the time being, let's leave that aside. I don't know any hedge fund managers.)

Payal Kadakia was studying to go to business school, but she took a break to found a dance company. She became frustrated with trying to find ballet classes online, so she created Class Pass, an app that lets you drop in to all sorts of classes. At the time of writing this, it's valued at over $1 billion.

Tobias Lütke was a German immigrant who wanted to stay in Canada but couldn't get a work visa. However, he could get an entrepreneur visa. He founded an online snowboard company, Snowdevil, but couldn't find a decent ecommerce platform to sell the snowboards on. A coder by trade, he coded a new online sales system. Eventually, they stopped selling snowboards and sold this platform instead, calling it Shopify.

Neither of these people are greedy or evil. They just created something the world needed, and were compensated for it. The company Jim Balsillie co-founded created tremendous value for the Canadian economy, launching the careers of thousands of students, and even now he uses his money and influence to fight for what's good for my country. As I write this, he has a net worth of $800 million. Is that an obscene amount of money? Is it a sign of capitalism gone wrong? I actually don't think so. His products improved the lives of millions.

(Now let me say, as an aside, that there are a lot of shitty things about capitalism, specifically American capitalism. Living in Canada, our capitalism still comes with universal health care and a comprehensive safety net. When I watch the U.S. talk about how giving people universal health care isn't realistic or watch them repeal parts of the Dodd-Frank Act that protect consumers, I want to scream.)

If you choose the path of entrepreneurship, there is one law that you need to understand. Add value and you will be compensated. Add more value and you will be compensated more. The more people you add value to, the more you will be compensated. Entrepreneurship is fundamentally an exchange of value for money, whether you're doing high-quality research for a company or giving hair cuts. My humanities degrees added no value to the world, and therefore I was not compensated. I scraped for government grants to underwrite my PhD passion and even thought I got them and got my research funded, I was not wealthy. Why? I didn't add much value.

My degree, frankly, was for the enrichment of myself — not of others. When I was sixteen, I worked sweeping floors at the local drugstore. The pharmacist I worked for offered to pay for my education. Yup, a free ride from beginning to end. The catch was, I'd have to be a pharmacist. He would pay for it, and then I'd have to come back to my small town and work for him for five years. It was an incredibly generous offer, but I hated science and math and wasn't interested in pharmacy, so I didn't take it. I don't regret it to this day. But that was a clear case of where my education would have had an immediate value to someone, so much so that he was willing to fund it.

The marketplace is simply an exchange of value. Money represents the value of a good or service. There are students who will never understand this. Some will mutter about neoliberalism and proclaim the evils of capitalism. But the marketplace works on a very simple principle. Solve someone's problem. Give someone something they need and charge for it. It's not morality or immorality; it's an exchange of value.

The more I meet entrepreneurs, the more I respect them. These are the people I look up to. They shape the world, work their asses off to make their vision come to life, and give the world what it needs. And they fail, a lot. A lot. They are creative and inspiring, and when they fall down, they stand back up and keep going.

* * *

So why would I include a chapter on entrepreneurs in this book? First of all, I must say that this is a reflection of my own personal journey, and entrepreneurship is a part of it. You don't need to become an entrepreneur; most PhDs won't be and that's okay. But some PhDs will, and consulting remains a great option for many of us. I want to show you what's there and share some of my thoughts and how my journey transpired.

When I worked for the government, people thought I'd arrived. I've already talked about why the role wasn't the right fit for what I loved to do, but it was also mind-numbingly boring. The average day I worked two to three hours. I saw that, with my PhD-honed skills, I could do things in half an hour that took others days to do. I could write a policy brief in a morning that would take someone else two weeks. No, I'm not unique. You could do it too. I was used to writing huge documents, so writing a nine-hundred-word policy brief was hardly rocket science.

I'd ask for more work, anything to do to make the day go faster. There wasn't any.

"Don't worry, there's going to be a lot of work coming your way!" my boss would chuckle.

It never came.

I was making $75,000 a year and getting interviews for jobs that paid over $100,000. But I was so bored. People sat around talking about their weekends and their pensions, and all I wanted was something to actually challenge me.

Around this time, I started to think about consulting again. I realized that if I were to be paid by the project I delivered rather than by the hours I sat in a chair, I could either make more or work less. Both of those sounded like great options. When I worked at the think tank the year before, I ran so fast all day that I never stopped. But now, at the government, I had a lot of time to think.

When I got offered a consulting role, it was a dream come true. I quit the government as fast as I could. People shook their heads and thought I was crazy, although I think some just wished they were brave enough to do what I had done.

Carolyne and I incorporated a company in January 2020. The company was structured as an umbrella to hold our various ventures, all of which are just in their infancy. Starting a company made me come alive. I learned more about myself and the world in weeks of owning a company than I learned in months working for the government. My brain buzzed with the complexity of it. There were always new things to learn. Then a global pandemic hit, and I couldn't network or sell. It got harder. But I've never once regretted leaving that terrible government job. I feel challenged and excited every day. Wherever this adventure takes me, I'm glad I'm on it.

Here are a couple more things I've learned during my brief time as an entrepreneur:

The world is made for businesses.

When you're an individual, you pay the government taxes off the top of your income, then you buy what you need with what you have left. When you're a business, you buy what you need first, then you pay your percentage of taxes on what's left. I don't know about your country or situation, but in Canada and the U.S., business taxes are much lower than income taxes. When I went to the bank to apply for a business credit card, I found out that I borrow money at 8 percent interest, compared to my personal credit card which is 18 percent. These are just little ways that the world works for businesses.

Entrepreneurship is a chance to earn what you're worth.

As I talked about in the last chapter, the middle-class logic smacked me on the side of the head when I started working. I was making $74,000 a year. After taxes I was bringing home around $50,000. This money had to support a family, pay our rent and bills, not to mention put a serious payment towards my student debt every month. The nice middle-class logic went right out the window. I was thirty-four years old. The only way I would ever retire at sixty-five with enough to live for the rest of my life would be to put away serious money every month — and there was nothing left by the time I paid everyone else. In fact, I calculated that I'd have to put away about $1,300 a month to hit $1 million by the time I retired, which is about what I'd need to live a lifestyle I wanted to live, especially with inflation over the next thirty-five years.

The middle-class ideals are problematic at the best of times, but for PhDs they are especially irrelevant. This logic works — when it works — based on time. Compound interest and small contributions take a lot of time to add up. When a twenty-five-year-old starts contributing to their pension, paying off their house, and building wealth, they might have something to show for it by the time they're sixty-five. If you finish your PhD at thirty-five, waste five years on adjunct positions and postdocs, and land a tenure-track gig when you're forty, you are far behind this twenty-five-year-old, especially if you have debt. Even if your job has a pension, by the time you pay down your student debt and start saving you're about twenty years behind the average twenty-five-year-old who jumps on the middle-class bandwagon. That was me. I saw that if I wanted to scrimp and save my way into the middle class it would take the rest of my life.

So, I made a high-risk/high-reward play at entrepreneurship. But let me tell you, it's not the easy way. It's really not. On top of conquering the various external forces in the world to come out on top, you need to conquer the person in the mirror. Sometimes that's the hardest. I still struggle with feelings of inadequacy. I suspect this might always be the case.

* * *

I used to think like the people in my hometown. I would look at the rich, successful entrepreneurs, running their own profitable business, driving whatever car they wanted and living in a big house, and say that they were "lucky." I don't say that anymore. Until you enter the ring of being an entrepreneur, you have no idea just how hard it is. It's not for everyone, nor should it be. At the end of the day, you don't go home and watch TV. You don't spend the weekends relaxing. You are always working or feeling like you should be working, especially at the beginning. There's a reason they call it the "hustle." It takes a ton of work. You have to repeatedly step out onto the ledge with no safety net, trusting yourself and your intuition to take the next step. You have to deal REPEATEDLY with failure. Disappointment is everywhere. The person who said they'd hire you walks away, and you're left with rent to pay and mouths to feed and it's all on you.

It's hard. Entrepreneurs are not lucky. They work their asses off. And they have no security. As one senior bureaucrat told me once, "There's nothing quite so nice as a paycheck." Yup, that can be true. So, if you're thinking of chasing an entrepreneurial dream, it's not for the faint of heart.

What did it come down to for me? Really there was one thing. I knew I'd never be happy working for someone else. I was a good employee on the outside. I had a good attitude (mostly). I did what I had to do. But somehow, in my first work outside of academia, I learned that I resent authority. I chafed working for other people. I craved freedom and I had my own dreams of world creation. I wanted to step into the arena and see what I was made of. I heard the voices of the naysayers. I heard people saying I was crazy. But I wanted to try.

I love Theodore Roosevelts' famous "Man in the Arena" speech. If you've never read it before, here it is (with language adapted for inclusivity):

> It is not the critic who counts; not the one who points out how the strong person stumbles, or where the doer of deeds could have done them better. The credit belongs to the one who is actually in the arena, whose face is marred by dust and sweat and blood; who strives valiantly; who errs, who comes short again and again, because there is no effort without error and shortcoming; but who does actually strive to do the deeds; who knows great enthusiasms, the great devotions; who spends themself in a worthy cause; who at the best knows in the end the triumph of high achievement, and who at the worst, if they fail, at least fail while daring greatly, so that their place shall never be with those cold and timid souls who neither know victory nor defeat.

I love this speech — one of the most powerful pieces of rhetoric I've ever read. I get chills when I read it. It inspires me to chase the very best version of myself that I can imagine and to ignore the haters. Because at the end of the day, it's not the critic who counts.

If you look at the gift that you want to give the world and there's no way to give it while working for someone else, then this might be your path. If your world-creating power takes you to the world of entrepreneurship, get ready to enter the arena. Because some of us need to be entrepreneurs against all odds. And while it's not easy, there's nothing else we can or will do. And that's okay.

12

IMAGINE YOUR LIFE

I've thrown a lot at you in the previous chapters. These are reflections, things I've learned along the way. I want to leave you with one final thing. If you've broken down the barriers in your mind you had about non-academic work and started to get an idea of how to create a career, this is the final step. It may even be the most important.

Imagine what's possible.

That's it. This seems like the most underwhelming piece of advice I can give you, but it's the one I cling to the most. Of all the things required to create a beautiful life for ourselves and a beautiful world for the people around us, imagination is vital.

When I first heard this from personal development speakers, I thought it was ridiculous. They'd say things like, "Imagine the future you want. Because if you can imagine it, you can build it." What a bunch of self-empowerment garbage, right?

Well, I have a confession to make. I've come to believe it too. Every morning, I sit in a chair in the darkness and I write down a description of what my future looks like. Over time, I've realized that I'm already progressing towards it faster than I realize.

Now, your imagination belongs to you alone, nobody else. So, when you sit to imagine the future, don't you dare paint someone else's view of what's good or possible across your mind. I spent too much of my life chasing what other people thought mattered instead of what I thought mattered. Don't do it.

Who are you? What is the world that you want to create?

Six months before I started writing this book, I was working for the government. I've already told you how miserable I was, how much the work didn't fit me, how much I hated commuting to work an hour each way. The bus always smelled like a mixture of fumes and cleaning products, and I spent most of my time on it trying not to barf.

I imagined living the life I lived in academia once again. I wanted to work from home and to have the freedom to travel, but this time I wanted to do it with lots of money in my bank account (and I didn't want to be anywhere near a university position). As I type this, the commuter bus just went by my window in a cloud of fumes. People are sitting on it, going into a job that they hate and already looking forward to the weekend — it's Monday. And I'm typing away at my laptop at my kitchen table in the darkness, a coffee next to me and one of my wonderful daughters — the one who's an early riser like me — is sitting near me reading. I have a company, a tiny little corporation that belongs to Carolyne and I and holds our various business interests. I have money in the bank from my consulting work.

Look at how far you've come! It's too easy to forget how much you've already achieved. You have— or are about to have — a PhD! Holy shit. That's not an achievement to be taken lightly. The funny thing about life is that we pretty quickly get used to things we only ever once dreamed about. There was that person you loved and never thought you could be with; now you roll your eyes at them because you've heard their jokes so many times. There was a scholarship you wanted, or a publication you dreamed about, or a class you desperately wanted to teach; now it's a line on your CV and you've forgotten all about it. Life is funny like this.

Never stop thinking about where you're going. Just as you've come this far, you can't even imagine where you'll get to. Or maybe you can. My dreams are changing all the time. I now envision a world where I get to do Roostervane full-time. Believe it or not, I haven't made a cent off of it as of writing this sentence. To be honest, I never expected to. It just started as a blog project to help people along the way. But this "little blog" has now become a potential business, even without customers yet. I just started by serving people and telling my story, and now thousands of people every week stumble across my virtual threshold, and the number is growing all the time.

I imagine a future where I close my consulting practice. I imagine getting paid to speak and write all the time. I see Roostervane helping millions of people around the world make sense of their degree, and my little stories on the blog earning me a comfortable living. That's just the beginning of my Big Hairy Audacious Goals, but for right now, I'll keep the rest to myself.

Wherever you feel you're at, sit down today and imagine your future. If you know you're leaving academia and you're scared, write for yourself an absolute dream scenario. Make a vision so damned cool you'd never ever dream of looking back. Do it to the best of your ability with your knowledge of the world. If you don't know the job title you want, just write the sort of career you want. Don't sell yourself short and lower the bar. Don't you dare think to yourself, *Oh that's too much. Let's make something more realistic.* This is your imagination, dammit! What's there is what's there, and you don't have to apologize for it.

Let me throw a few more buzzwords at you and tell you why, even though each is overused, I think they are really important and vital to creating the world you imagine.

Focus

The things you focus on become your reality. I've heard this from so many different personal development people that I can't even attribute it properly, but I think it's true. Remember narrative psychology from chapter five? When we wake up in the morning and think, *There's nothing I can do* or *I'll never have a career I love,* that becomes your truth. You'll find evidence that affirms it and accept it. When you wake up and think, *I know I can do something great. I just need to figure out what that is,* you'll find yourself focusing on that instead.

If you're looking at leaving academia and you think, *I'll never be happy doing anything else* or *no employer will want me,* those become your reality. Each job rejection you get confirms your belief, and you're headed towards a dark place. Remember Erin in chapter four? She got a job waiting tables as her first role out of academia and eventually became a marketing director. She told herself, *I'm a hard worker. I've gotten jobs before, and I know I can do it again.* She focused on this instead of the things that sucked about her current place in life. And she built a great career that she loves.

Make sure you focus on the good instead of the bad. Focus on where you are successful, and what you can do, and look for places to connect it into the world.

Vision

Do you know what most people do when they look for a job? They search for phrases like, "What type of job can I get with my degree?" They look for job postings that look like they might fit them and try to apply. Now, we all do this at some point. Occasionally we all have to work jobs that aren't the perfect fit for us. Sometimes we just need a paycheck.

HOWEVER, a life needs vision. If you don't define your vision, you'll wander down whatever path opens up for you. Which is what most people do. There are even people in tenure-track jobs who wandered in without ever thinking about whether its what they really want. And yup, they're miserable too. Like I said earlier, I get the emails and DMs. When you go where life takes you instead of where you want to go, you inevitably wake up when you're fifty and wonder how you got to where you are. You realize that you don't want to be there.

I love the famous dialogue with the Cheshire Cat from Alice in Wonderland:

> *"Would you tell me, please, which way I ought to go from here?"*
> *"That depends a good deal on where you want to get to," said the Cat.*
> *"I don't much care where—" said Alice.*
> *"Then it doesn't matter which way you go," said the Cat.*
> *" so long as I get somewhere," Alice added as an explanation.*
> *"Oh, you're sure to do that," said the Cat, "if you only walk long*

enough."[20]

This is the attitude too many people have about life. They talk about "doors opening," and "the next step," without any idea of where they want to go. (Of course, there are times when we need to take the next step without having a full vision of the future.) Your future will be best if you decide what it is rather than waiting for someone to decide for you. Don't be the person waiting for someone to come and change their lives. Don't be the poor person buying lottery tickets hoping their life will change. Be the one building your own life according to your own roadmap.

Define your vision. Get it as specific as you can. If you don't have a specific career in mind, set your vision according to the type of work you want to do. I want to help thousands of people who are lost after their degrees turn them into an amazing life. That's my vision. It's a bit blurry at times. I don't always know what it looks like, but I DO know when I'm doing things that are not leading me down the right path.

Keep coming back to your vision. Revisit it. I choose to write it and rewrite it every morning to embed it into my mind. Find a way to clarify your vision and start living towards it.

Drive

What moves you? Where do you get the will to keep going, even when you want to quit? Start to figure out your own psychology and how you work to learn how to keep yourself moving. For most of us, operating at top-level means getting enough sleep, living on a schedule, drinking enough water, eating right, and exercising. This all seems like a tall order if you're doing none of the above, but try to find the little things that will make you work better and tweak them.

Hunger

What do you want out of this life? Don't be afraid to nurture some big dreams that propel you forwards. People around you might get intimidated by your hunger. They might say, "You need to be realistic," or, "Be thankful for what you have."

Yes, be thankful for what you have. But also, never stop being hungry to get more out of life, whatever that looks like for you. More freedom. More influence. More helping people. Don't try to silence your hunger. Feed it. And never apologize for it.

Work Ethic

It's easy to get excited about your dream for a day and then forget it the next. It's incredibly difficult to keep working towards it day after day, when it feels like all life is stacked against you. When your parents or friends tell you it's crazy, it's way easier to take the safe way. But you already know this, don't you? Otherwise you wouldn't have done a PhD. The real world takes a lot of self-discipline too. When you dedicate yourself to your vision, it's unlikely that anyone will go with you. You'll have to go there alone. It's you who will get up early and go to bed late. You'll be the one who's working when everyone else is watching The Bachelor. The bigger your vision, the more work it's going to take. And it will be a lonely walk. Get ready.

Productivity

Learn to be productive, not just busy. It's easy to be busy and feel like you're doing something. I see students doing it all the time, pouring hours and hours into their research without ever producing anything. They spend days and months going down rabbit trails that never lead anywhere. Productivity requires a clear goal to work towards. It has a clear measure of success, so that you can tell how far down the road you are towards your goal.

If finishing your PhD is the goal for you still, get it done. Stop procrastinating or following other trails, and pump that damned thing out. If you're done or almost done with your degree and are now working on this thing called life, define your vision so that you know you're being productive. (If you've never worked with SMART goals, this is a good time to Google them.)

Just a note, I think some people are hesitant to finish their PhD because they are uncertain about what is coming next. The fear of what happens once we complete that degree can hold us back from finishing. This might be fear of facing a hostile and unfruitful academic job market. It might be fear of having to reinvent yourself in non-academic work. Acknowledge your fear if you have it. But also, pull the band aid off.

* * *

One of the most soul-destroying things about striking out of academia is that we're tempted to think that we have to take our big, lofty, audacious dreams and clip them. We imagine that our accomplishments will be less. Our impact will be diminished. And we'll be confined to a humdrum life that's underwhelming.

Nothing could be further from the truth. PhDs are often, by nature, driven individuals with big goals and ideas. Getting passed over for an academic career doesn't take that away. You might be hurt for a while. You might go through the darkness. In fact, you probably will. But your powerful spirit is not just going to be tamed by disappointment. It's not going to give up because of what you perceive as a failure.

You'll take a breath, and then you'll begin to look at the world again. You'll look at the cards you've been dealt, and you'll begin to pick up the pieces. Chances are, you won't quit until you build a life that you love. And when you find yourself off track, you'll make the correction.

In the second half of this book, I've given you some broad lessons that have been valuable for me. These are not a step-by-step blueprint for building your future, but they do give you a sense of where to start when you're lost.

1. Find your definition of success.

Figure out what success means to you and identify the types of work that would make you feel successful. Because that will help you to redefine where you want to go and show you what's important to you.

2. Develop your leadership flame.

This means developing the ability to make clear decisions about your own life and chasing the things that mean the most to you. It also means learning to become a leader in the worlds you occupy, and especially the work world, because PhDs are too educated not to be leaders. This doesn't mean that you have to be the boss, but it does mean that you'll be able to take ownership of your work and lead in whatever way is necessary.

3. Grow your network.

Recognize that your success depends on other people, and there's nothing wrong with that. Networking is not as hard as you think, and everyone who's growing a career should take it seriously. Networking will open you up to job possibilities you didn't even know were there and will expand your reputation.

4. Build your brand.

People get an impression from you whether you like it or not, and with the online world, you can build a great brand and reach thousands of people for free! Don't take that lightly. Whatever domain you're in, become the person known for excellence in that thing and people will come to you.

5. Learn about money

If growing your wealth is important to you, or even if you just want to be paid what you're worth, learn about money. Educate yourself about personal finance and stamp out the poverty mindset and bad attitudes that will hold you back in your journey. Imagine a day where you could go out to a restaurant without putting your account into overdraft or being afraid of being declined!

6. Consider entrepreneurship (if it's your thing)

While it's not for everyone, some PhDs might find their calling as entrepreneurs, creating something in the marketplace. If you're someone who has a vision of entrepreneurship, do what it takes to chase it and get you there. And, even if you're not, develop an entrepreneurial attitude so that you can become a valuable *intrapreneur,* someone who brings creativity and innovation to the company where you work.

* * *

I think Plato's allegory of the cave is one of the most interesting metaphors for the human condition. If you've never read it, the basic story is that there are a group of people who are chained to a cave wall. The only reality they've ever known is the shadows on the wall in front of them from a window high above their heads. They watch those shadows dance and it's all they know. They think it's the real world.

One day, someone gets out of the cave. They come blinking into the sunlight and see the world for what it is. They go back into the cave to try to explain reality to the people left behind, but those people have no idea what they're talking about.

The thing I find most interesting about Plato's allegory of the cave is not that it's a perfect picture for human enlightenment. Far be it from me to disagree with Plato. But what is most interesting to me is that every single human being who hears the allegory of the cave thinks it's about them. We all think we're enlightened. When I was religious, the cave was used as a metaphor for spiritual awakening. I later heard atheists use it to describe their own awakening. University professors used it to describe education and how it wakes us from slumber. PhD students use it to describe the world they've left behind, that they don't want to go back to. Business owners use it as a metaphor for the entrepreneurial life. Globetrotters use it to describe the folks who never travel.

So, I actually think the allegory of the cave isn't a metaphor for human enlightenment at all. I think it's a better depiction of how humans *think* about our own enlightenment. The cave isn't about awakening. It's about confirmation bias. But the metaphor also helps with the construction of human communities. I'm not going down a rabbit hole here, but virtually every human community I've ever belonged to, big or small, needed to justify their existence and uniqueness. This type of metaphor — that we're unique in our enlightenment and view of the world — is a constituting rationale for a lot of human organizations, from offices, to religious institutions, to academia. Everybody wants to think they've left the Matrix.

Real life can't work like this. Enlightenment is bullshit. We grow and learn. We're never enlightened. I've had no less than ten "leaving the cave moments" in my life, each felt more real than the last. Leaving academia was one of them, where I stepped blinking into the sunlight and felt sorry for all those left behind. Then I left the office job for entrepreneurship and once again felt myself blinking in a whole new brightness. Who knows what the next one will be?

There is no one point of awakening. Ideally, you'll be more enlightened tomorrow than you are today. There is only growth and movement, progressive revelations about how the world works, and what you want from it. True enlightenment is being willing to take the journey of being a human. It's the ability to step blinking into the sun again and again, no matter how uncomfortable it may make you, to fully live the life you've been given. It's stepping out of your comfort zone, your cave, time and time again. Each time the cave wall begins to feel good on your back and the shadows on the wall in front of you feel too real, run into the light again. Because enlightenment isn't a destination. It's a way of life.

So, at the end of a book written for the most highly-educated people on earth, I have one last piece of advice.

Wake up.

Then wake up again.

Then wake up again.

Keep on waking up until, like a character from *Inception*, you forget whether you're awake or asleep.

Each moment of awakening is a signal that you have learned a new way of being, a new way of seeing the world. In these moments of learning, we cross a threshold and become something new too. The more you become, the more you have to give the world. The more you give, the more you become and the more beautiful life is. It's a wonderful cycle.

So, if you're just waking up from a long dream, welcome. Step into the light. Your journey is just beginning.

If you are in the process of leaving, you probably won't have everything figured out.

It's hard to dream a new dream right as your old one is dying. If you are giving up on a tenure-track dream, you likely won't have a fully formed dream waiting to take its place. You just need to start moving. Take some steps into the future. It won't make sense at first. It will probably feel awful and gross. But eventually you'll come to the place you can dream again. And once you do, make sure you dream even bigger than the tenure-track you. Don't compress your imagined future. Tell yourself that you have something even bigger to do.

I dream of seeing thousands of PhDs step into leadership positions and use their intellect and skills to run this world. I imagine industries transformed, new technologies developed, and new companies and non-profits built by educated innovators who are brave enough to step out of academia and start again. I think of the problems that these minds could solve: poverty, climate change, waste. All this is possible, but it takes a generation of PhDs who are brave enough to take a chance on themselves and create a life that matches their ambition.

So, I wish you well on your journey to building the life of your dreams with your degree. I'm excited to see where it takes you.

Notes

LOST AND FOUND

1   National Center for Science and Engineering Statistics, National Science Foundation, "Doctorate Recipients from U.S. Universities: 2018," Survey of Earned Doctorates (Alexandria, VA: National Science Foundation, December 2019), https://ncses.nsf.gov-/pubs/nsf20301/; Statistics Canada, "Table 37-10-0031-01 National Graduates Survey (NGS), Postsecondary Graduates, by Location of Residence at Interview and Level of Study," https://doi.org/10.25318/3710003101-eng.

2   "Infographic: The Countries With The Most Doctoral Graduates." n.d. Statista Infographics. https://www.statista.com/chart/7272/the-countries-with-the-most-doctoral-graduates/.

3   David Walters, David Zarifa, and Brittany Etmanski, "Employment in Academia: To What Extent Are Recent Doctoral Graduates of Various Fields of Study Obtaining Permanent Versus Temporary Academic Jobs in Canada?," *Higher Education Policy*, February 11, 2020, https://doi.org/10.1057/s41307-020-00179-w; While I couldn't find clear numbers for the U.S., Andrew Jacob Cuff's estimate of 10-25 percent seems accurate, see, "An Academic Lottery or a Meritocracy?" *Inside Higher Ed,* May 3, 2017, https://www.insidehighered.com/advice/2017/05/03/phds-need-real-data-how-potential-employers-make-hiring-decisions-essay. These numbers are from prior to the 2020 pandemic.

4   Joanna R. Frye and Amy P. Fulton, "Mapping the Growth and Demographics of Managerial and Professional Staff in Higher Education," *New Directions for Higher Education* 2020, no. 189 (2020): 7–23.

5   "The Mental Health of PhD Researchers Demands Urgent Attention." *Nature* 575 (2019): 257–58. https://doi.org/10.1038/d41586-019-03489-1.

6   Paul Taylor et al., "Is College Worth It? College Presidents, Public Assess Value, Quality and Mission of Higher Education," Social & Demographic Trends (Washington: PewResearch-Center, May 2011), Chapter 5; Statistics Canada. Table 37-10-0035-01 National Graduates Survey (NGS), estimated gross annual earnings of postsecondary graduates working full time at interview, by location of residence at interview, level of study and sex

7   Daniel Munro and Jessica Edge, "Inside and Outside the Academy: Valuing and Preparing PhDs for Careers" (Ottawa: The Conference Board of Canada, 2015), https://www.conferenceboard.ca/e-Library/document.aspx?did=7564.

WHAT CAN YOU DO WITH A PHD?

8   Lynn McAlpine and Cheryl Amundsen, *Post-PhD Career Trajectories: Intentions, Decision-Making and Life Aspirations* (London: Palgrave Macmillan, 2016).

THE DARKNESS

9   Peter L. Berger and Thomas Luckmann, *The Social Construction of Reality: A Treatise in the Sociology of Knowledge* (London: Penguin UK, 199 [1966]); Peter Berger and Stanley Pullberg, "Reification and the Sociological Critique of Consciousness," *History and Theory* 4, no. 2 (January 1, 1965): 196–211, https://doi.org/10.2307/2504151.

YOU'RE NOT WORTHLESS

10   https://www.theglobeandmail.com/report-on-business/careers/business-education/want-a-degree-with-that-mcdonalds-training-is-now-a-path-to-a-college-diploma/article31454909/

THE LIFE OF REINVENTION

11   Dan P. McAdams and Kate C. McLean, "Narrative Identity," *Current Directions in Psychological Science* 22(3) (2013): 233–38.

12   Dan P. McAdams and Kate C. McLean, "Narrative Identity," 236.

13   "The Deloitte Global Millennial Survey 2019: Societal Discord and Technological Transformation Create a 'Generation Disrupted,'" 2019, https://www2.deloitte.com/content/dam/Deloitte/global/Documents/About-Deloitte/deloitte-2019-millennial-survey.pdf.

14   Ben Miller et al., "Addressing the $1.5 Trillion in Federal Student Loan Debt" (Center for American Progress, June 2019), https://www.americanprogress.org/issues/education-postsecondary/reports/2019/06/12/470893/addressing-1-5-trillion-federal-student-loan-debt/.

LEADERSHIP

15   Frank J. Sulloway, *Born to Rebel: Birth Order, Family Dynamics, and Creative Lives* (Diane Publishing Company, 2001); cf. Julia M. Rohrer, Boris Egloff, and Stefan C. Schmukle, "Examining the Effects of Birth Order on Personality," *Proceedings of the National Academy of Sciences* 112, no. 46 (November 17, 2015): 14224–29, https://doi.org/10.1073/pnas.1506451112.

NETWORKING

16   First published as, Pierre Bourdieu, "Ökonomisches Kapital, kulturelles Kapital, soziales Kapital," in *Soziale Ungleichheiten* (ed. Reinhard Kreckel; Soziale Welt, Sonderheft 2; Göttingen, 1983), 183–98; Pierre Bourdieu, "The Forms of Capital," in *Readings in Economic Sociology*, ed. Nicole Woolsey Biggart, Blackwell Readers in Sociology (John Wiley & Sons, 2002), 286.

17   Another early proponent of social capital was James S. Coleman, "Social Capital in the Creation of Human Capital," *American Journal of Sociology* 94 (1988), 95–120.

BUILDING YOUR BRAND

18 Douglas Kruger, *Own Your Industry* (Cape Town: Penguin Random House South Africa, 2014.)

MONEY

19 "Tenured/Tenure-Track Faculty Salaries - HigherEdJobs." n.d. Www.Higheredjobs.Com. https://www.higheredjobs.com/salary/salaryDisplay.cfm?SurveyID=46.

IMAGINE YOUR LIFE

20 Lewis Carroll, *Alice's Adventures in Wonderland* (New York: Macmillan, 1920), 89–90.

Printed in Great Britain
by Amazon

44908013R00097